D1435612

ANIMAL
OMENS

About the Author

Victoria Hunt (California) has studied metaphysics and earth spirituality for over twelve years. A third-level Reiki master and member of the British Druid Order, she teaches Celtic-based earth-centered spirituality out of her studio, Grove of the Red Hawk, and has organized and led Celtic celebrations and rituals.

ANIMAL OMENS

Victoria Hunt

Llewellyn Publications
Woodbury, Minnesota

First Edition
First Printing, 2008

Cover design by Lisa Novak
Interior book design by Joanna Willis
Interior illustrations © Shutterstock

Llewellyn is a registered trademark of Llewellyn Worldwide, Ltd.

Quotation on page xiii from Joaquin Miller, *Life Amongst the Modocs: Unwritten History* (London: Richard Bentley and Sons, 1873).

Quotation on page 130 from Anna Franklin, *Familiars: Animal Powers of Britain,* page 140 (Milverton, England: Capall Bann Publishing, 1997), Auton Farm, Milverton, Somerset TX4 1NE, www.capallbann.co.uk, ISBN 978-1-898307-85-3. Used with permission.

Library of Congress Cataloging-in-Publication Data
Hunt, Victoria, 1953–
  Animal omens / by Victoria Hunt. — 1st ed.
    p. cm.
  ISBN 978-0-7387-1377-9
  1. Animals—Miscellanea. 2. Human-animal communication—Miscellanea.
3. Omens. I. Title.
  BF1623.A55H87 2008
  133'.259—dc22

                                                                            2008005858

Llewellyn Worldwide does not participate in, endorse, or have any authority or responsibility concerning private business transactions between our authors and the public.
  All mail addressed to the author is forwarded but the publisher cannot, unless specifically instructed by the author, give out an address or phone number.
  Any Internet references contained in this work are current at publication time, but the publisher cannot guarantee that a specific location will continue to be maintained. Please refer to the publisher's website for links to authors' websites and other sources.

Llewellyn Publications
A Division of Llewellyn Worldwide, Ltd.
2143 Wooddale Drive, Dept. 978-0-7387-1377-9
Woodbury, MN 55125-2989, U.S.A.
www.llewellyn.com

Printed in the United States of America

For the Old Ones, and the Spirits that teach me.

CONTENTS

ACKNOWLEDGEMENTS

I WOULD LIKE TO THANK all of those who were willing to let me share their animal encounters: Barbara, Kathy, Dan, Sunnee, Jan, Dave, Howard, John, and a person who chose to remain anonymous. Without you, this book would not have been complete. I also wish to thank my father for raising me with a love and respect for the land and helping me to find vision beyond the ordinary. You are a perfect example of what connection truly is. Love you, Dad.

INTRODUCTION

THE NINETEENTH-CENTURY POET JOAQUIN MILLER described the mountain as "lonely as God, and white as a winter moon." All I know is that of all the places to choose to begin a journey, this was the best place to start. I believe it wasn't just luck that caused me to be born there—I think it was providence, for I had a path to follow, and this was the beginning.

I arrived in a small town that sits at the foot of the fifth-highest mountain peak in California, Shasta. Shasta is known for its spiritual vortex and is one of the great power spots on the planet. Many Native tribes, as well as New Agers, hold it as sacred. My family only lived there five years, but that was long enough for me to have my roots firmly grounded in the spirituality and love of the land.

As time moved on and I grew up, I found more and more that my views of life and living were markedly different from the mainstream, the normal consensus of most people. I knew things others did not, and I didn't know how to explain it. I saw different levels of reality, talked with people who were invisible to most humans, and had a love for solitude that some called reclusive. Not that I didn't enjoy friends, and parties, and most things young girls enjoyed—I really tried hard to fit in, but I always felt like an outsider. It was a tough time for a sensitive who wanted to belong.

Through it all, I always cherished my time in the wild places of nature, for nature sustained me, accepting me just as I was. That was more than I received at the time from humanity. But, as with most of humanity—I wasn't blind to human frailties—I got lost along the way, lost my sense of self, of the real me and what I wanted in life. I was still trying hard to fit in and "walk the talk" that had been instilled in me by the society I grew up in—a society enmeshed in the Vietnam War, space travel, color television, freeways, smog, and keeping up with the Joneses. I wanted to believe that the ways of that society were right, but I just couldn't shake the idea that things were going *way* wrong—until my big turnaround.

It just took one decision, one small step off the treadmill, and I started to wake up, to regain what had been there all along but had been shoved down behind my efforts to conform.

It was in the mid-1990s that my life took a turn back toward where I had first begun my journey—my life as a member of a family of hereditary "ultra-sensitives," people whose senses are heightened beyond the normal. It wasn't a shift back in locale, but a shift back in consciousness, back to my connection with nature and the land. It was a shift that saved my life.

My first real reawakening began when I took up walking to relieve stress. Every day I walked down the sidewalk past a huge Valley Oak tree. I appreciated its beauty but didn't think much more about it than that. As weeks turned into months, which turned into years, the oak and I forged a relationship that was as solid and strong as he was. His name was King Oak, and I delighted in seeing him on a daily basis, for he was full of light and goodness, and he would subtly prick my far memory of what and who I had been. He was bursting with life of his own and all the creatures who dwelt in his branches. It was he who woke me up. And then, suddenly, it seemed, he was gone—cut down in the name of progress.

A housing development sprang up on two acres of richly wooded sacred land, and King Oak was in the way of that progress. When I found out what was planned, I tried to save him every way I knew how, but in the end "progress" won. I was devastated. My rock, my anchor, was no more, and I felt I had been set adrift on a seemingly endless sea.

I wept bitterly at his passing, but inside me, things were stirring.

Over time I came to realize—and remember—that even though I could no longer visibly see King Oak, he was not necessarily gone from me. The loss of form is not necessarily the loss of life or existence. We could still talk anytime. So I took this insight with me as I forged myself a new path and new relationships with nature. I wandered farther and deeper into the woods, remembering, learning, and growing stronger on my earth-centered path.

Then, one warm summer evening in August, I rediscovered my ability to converse with spiritual beings. I had officiated at a small gathering of women celebrating the Celtic festival of the first fruits of the harvest, Lughnasadh, in honor of the Celtic god Lugh. During the festival, as we tried to maintain a note of seriousness, mishaps kept occurring, one after another. Some were frustrating, some were funny, but all were out of the ordinary and unexplainable. My spirit guide, Balthazar, made his presence known to me then, whispering in my ear and making me forget what I was saying, then having a good laugh about it: a joke on me. He was my spirit guide, my brother, he said, from another time and another place, assisting me along my life path. We haven't parted since. He appears several times in the pages of this book.

Balthazar went with me into the woods and taught me more about life and living among the energies of nature. As we wandered, I learned a lot about animals and animal omens. I found that the more animals I encountered the more I understood, and the more I understood the more I appreciated them. I could often relate an encounter to a situation or emotion that was occurring in my life.

I wondered whether other people I knew were having similar experiences. So I asked around among friends and acquaintances and found that many of them had also had an animal encounter which, when they stopped to think about it, could be linked with an emotion, problem, or situation that was occurring in their own lives, or perhaps had already occurred. Then a personal spiritual experience prompted me to compile these stories of animal encounters—my own and others'—into a collection, hoping to help people reconnect with the world of nature.

Our ancestors lived and worked with animals on real and personal levels. They knew animals' importance in their lives. They recognized that animals weren't lower than humans on some evolutionary scale, but that we all come from the world of nature and are connected through an energetic link with creation, with Spirit—however we choose to view Spirit. Through experience, our ancestors learned to communicate with animals in order to gain knowledge and bring balance and healing to themselves and their tribe or clan members.

Animals and animal omens can provide insights and guidance, teaching us how to use our intuition, senses, and powers of observation more acutely to gain a clearer picture of how life works. By taking the time to look past ordinary everyday reality, you'll discover that the answers to life's questions await in the ancient wisdom of animals. By being willing and open, you can be ready for an animal to come to you with the guidance you're looking for. For you don't go in search of them; they seek you out to offer their own form of wisdom and insight, and it will come through loud and clear.

This book is a compilation of my own stories of animal encounters, together with stories from nine other people: Jan, Kathy, John, Barbara, Dave, Howard, Dan, Sunnee, and a person who chose to remain anonymous. All took place in our own state of California, except for the Horse story, which took place in the northern Nevada desert region. Each story also includes a commentary on the omen and the powers that the animal holds. Together, they show how we can blend our physical and spiritual lives together into one awareness, thus regaining what has been lost to us through years of neglect and disconnection from the source of all existence—the world of nature.

Life and knowledge are continually unfolding, bringing with them better versions of being. I hope these stories can in some way help you, the reader, the spiritual seeker, to evolve into those better versions. Some of the stories are very personal in nature, shared out of a desire to assist in understanding the humanity we all have in common. Please read them in the light of that desire, and know they come from the heart.

May the Divine Energies go with you on your journey through life, and may you always hold open a space for them to reach you.

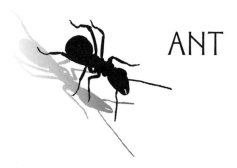

ANT

THE BLACK ASPHALT SIZZLING IN the sun contrasted sharply with the cool, shady green of the leafy oaks by the edge of the road. Around here in July, 105 degrees is pretty mild, and mornings hold no relief. From where I stood, I saw shadows of wings shifting on the ground's rocky surface. Birds were moving in the branches above me.

Then, in a sudden display of tiny opaque wings, hundreds of flying insects rose up in a mass from the ground toward the sky. I wasn't sure what kind they were, but they flew higher and higher, forming a swirling funnel of continuous activity that reached all the way into the lobed green leafage of the oaks.

I stood spellbound for a solid five minutes, and the funnel of bugs never ceased. Curiosity took over, so I moved closer. Hundreds more insects on the ground were crawling over each other for their turn at lift-off. I wasn't the only one watching: three blue jays next to me were as fascinated as I, only I had already eaten my breakfast, and they were just enjoying theirs.

Then I looked up. The dark gray shadows that were cast on the ground took on color. Blue wings and the light gray bellies of more blue jays were scooping and diving after the flying funnel. And dragonflies, too. It must have been pot-luck to the nth degree. Nature in action.

I went home and called my entomologist friend. Flying ants, he said. Right time of year for the mating ritual. Do the dance, mate, come back to earth, males die, females form the new colony. That's fair in the insect world.

That morning started my insect education. Nature can teach you pretty much anything you need to know: just watch and listen.

Victoria

Omen

Ants are social insects that live in large communities, working for the good of the colony. These colonies consist of one or two queens, many workers, and soldiers who guard and protect the nests. Ants are industrious, disciplined, patient, and skilled at building and organizing.

As an omen, Ant can signal the start of a busy period in your life. A project, artistic endeavor, career, or relationship may begin to move forward. Remember to stay centered and focused on what is coming into being. Patience, and learning patience, will be interwoven into this forward movement—patience with ourselves and others we meet along our way.

Patience can be defined as the will or ability to wait or endure without complaint. So it's not only being patient that applies here, it's also the ability to be so without voicing displeasure or annoyance.

By learning about the right way to handle busy periods in our lives, we also learn how to extend that out into our community and the world at large. Look to Ant and his discipline and patience as the example to follow.

BEAVER

EARLY MORNING BY THE CREEK. I pause and watch, munching on a handful of breakfast cereal, its taste sweet in my mouth. Something slowly moving upstream arouses my curiosity, and feelings of a surreal nature slip through me. Otter or raccoon?

Wrong on both counts. A large adult beaver flips over onto its back to watch me watching it as it paddles by. I notice a silver-dollar-sized chunk gone out of its tail. Must have had a tangle with something. The beaver continues its foray up the creek, one eye keeping me in sight. I watch in total amazement: this is my first beaver sighting along my edge of the world. Then it's gone, higher up the creek.

Later in the day I share this advent with some old canyon friends.

"Beaver on Little Butte Creek? Yeah, right." Last sighting was thirty years ago.

A few months later: another sighting. I feel validation.

Five years later: willow trees on the bank start to disappear. Another year passes, and more trees fall. You can hear their incisors cutting through the trunks at night. *Crash!* Dogs bark. My friends are back in full force, building their home.

I am, too. We're busy creatures.

John

Omen

Beavers are large rodents with chisel-like teeth, webbed hind feet, and flat broad tails. They are skilled at building dams out of mud and twigs, making their homes along rivers and creeks.

Beavers work as a team as they fell trees and construct their homes. This reflects the ability to work together to achieve an end, recognizing that not all things can or should be done alone. Sometimes you need to divvy up the workload.

If Beaver swims your way, stop and ask yourself if you have been keeping distance between yourself and the people in your life who might be able to help you out in a situation, find a solution to a problem, or just be there to offer emotional support. If you've been playing the recluse, now is the time to integrate back into society, to turn back to those who love and support you—your friends and family.

Beaver is telling you that there is time for solitude and time to share the power of living. Now is the time to share.

BUTTERFLY

ON THIS PLEASANT DAY IN February, we're blessed with a beautiful new winter morning. The sunlight sifts through the cloud cover whenever the wind blows a different direction. Sometimes the clouds shift so fast, only a brief hint of light comes from above. The temperature has risen the last few days, making it warm enough to be June.

Little white flowers have popped up on the Miner's lettuce, and the grass is fresh and new, springtime green dappled with tiny drops of dew. I run my hands along the green surface, purifying them in this early-morning moisture, then bring them to my face. Water is sacred to the Earth Mother, so by purifying my hands and face I claim her as my own and rededicate myself to her. It is her breath that has sent the moisture clinging to the fragile flowers and blades of grass. It is life-giving, this breath of hers.

I get the impression that I am to walk a different direction through the trees today. And as I do so, fate steps in. Just off the path I stop to look at a hawthorn tree starting to bud out—they are always first, and lovely in their white adornment when flowering. Next to this tree loved by the faeries is an oak. My eyes catch sight of something winged clinging to the trunk, so I step closer.

It's a butterfly, one I've not seen before, dark maroon-brown with a golden border edged by small blue buttons. A beautiful creature, with its fuzzy dark body and velvety wings. I want to reach out and touch it, for it looks so soft, but I don't. Instead I just stand gazing at its rich splendor. I hadn't realized butterflies come out so early in the year. Now I'm excited to run home to my bookshelf to find out what this child of nature is.

Saying my thanks, I hurry off to read about butterflies in my insect book, as my curiosity has been aroused by this unusual sighting in the last stage of winter.

What did I discover that day? I was reminded that there are some amazing things in the world around us if we'll just listen to our impressions and follow where they lead. If we do, gifts may be revealed that can enhance our life's journey and make us glad we agreed to the trip—gifts like butterflies.

Victoria

Omen

The mourning cloak is one of the first butterflies to be seen when the weather turns warm and the days sunny. Mourning Cloaks can live a full year, while most butterflies live only three months. Their blackish-brown to maroon-colored wings have a golden yellow edging bordered by brilliant blue dots.

The butterfly is a symbol of the soul in flight from the body after death, beautiful in its true nature, unhampered by its earthly form. The butterfly has also been seen as a shape-shifter, able to transform itself into something other than its present form as it goes from egg to caterpillar to chrysalis to butterfly.

Butterfly can teach us about transformation. About change and how we can change in beauty and joy, for change doesn't need to be a negative experience—there is beauty in change.

If Butterfly has flown into your life, ask yourself if you need to undergo a change of some sort. Maybe in your relationships with others, your living arrangements, or in your thinking? Whichever it might be, a change is at hand. Stay open for renewal and be prepared for this change to make itself known, for you are forewarned, and so forewarned you can be ready and willing to go where change leads.

Every change can be viewed as a growing, expanding, learning experience. All life is change; nothing remains the same. But Butterfly can help you with the transformation that is coming. Just look for the beauty that it holds, and embrace it willingly.

CAT

"Whose baby is that crying?" I said out loud to myself. "What a mournful sound."

It was a Monday, a day my antique shop was closed. I'd left something there the previous day and now I was back to pick it up. If I hadn't needed it for an appointment that day, I wouldn't have bothered.

As soon as I stepped out of my car, I heard the crying. I looked around, wondering where the sound was coming from. Then I noticed a small black kitten trying to scale the front of the building: it was her little voice—such a sad, pitiful cry.

I scooped her off the wall, trying to calm her down and wondering what I was going to do with her. I couldn't leave her there: she was tiny, not more than eight weeks old. But I couldn't take her home either; I already had five cats. I opted for the Humane Society: maybe they could find a good family for her. So I went inside and made the phone call.

At first the answer was yes, they'd be happy to take her. But when I gave my address—I live in the country—the answer changed. They only took city cats. Sorry, no. That left me no other choice, so home we went, and I placed her in my backyard until I could return.

"If she's there when I get home, she's meant to be mine," I thought, and with that I left for my appointment. Sure enough, when I got home there she was, sitting on the step waiting for me as if she'd done it many times before.

I called her Lucky—for her and for me. Black cats are considered unlucky; she was anything but. With the twist of fate that brought us together she proved that superstition wrong. She had been rescued and I was given an extraordinary experience. She was my lucky angel.

Seven or eight years later, as I was sitting at my piano pounding out the only song I knew, feeling heartbroken and crying over a current problem, out of nowhere, up jumped Lucky onto the piano keys. She walked across the keyboard to me, the notes ringing out softly with each step. Then she looked up and placed both paws around my neck, nuzzling my chin with her face. It was at that moment that I knew my mother's spirit had come back to visit me, manifested in my cat Lucky.

My mother was a wonderful person, and we shared a special bond. So it came as no surprise that she'd travel back to visit periodically through my cat. She had loved cats, and our household always included cats when I was growing up.

From that point on, Lucky slept on the chair that had belonged to my mother; she'd lie there purring contentedly for hours. At night she started sleeping wrapped around my head or flat out on my arm with her little face next to mine and our breaths blending into one, leaving me with an incredible sense of peace.

Lucky and I shared a rich and happy fifteen years together, then she passed on. In the end I could see why she had chosen me to be her companion, for she had important things to teach and I had the opportunity to feel my mother near again and partake in something uniquely special. I miss them both, but I know that someday we will be reunited.

Barbara

Omen

Through the ages, cats have been associated with the spiritworld, held in high esteem for their ability to see and work in close proximity with the worlds of both the living and the departed.

In certain cultures it's believed that the souls of the departed can move into a cat and reside there until the cat dies. Then the cat carries the souls into the afterlife to await rebirth. That makes cats conduits between the physical and the spiritual worlds, holding both open simultaneously.

Cats are very sensitive to subtleties around them because their hearing, eyesight, and sense of smell are so acute. Hence their connection to those departed and to the spirit-world. They can sense when the Otherworld portal has opened, and stay perfectly still purring contentedly for long periods of time. The cat has also been seen as able to make prophecies and predict the weather.

Cats are very reserved, independent, and confident in themselves. They have great patience and are perfectly content to wait however long it takes to get what they desire.

If Cat has come your way, look for the magical to manifest but be patient in the waiting, for it will happen in its own time and in its own way. Be aware of any sign that comes while you are going about your life. Be quiet and listen, see and smell what is around you, and stay attuned to your senses. You are being told to hold open a place for the special to happen, and it will.

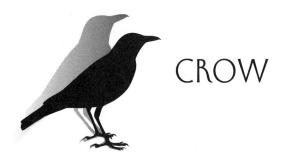

CROW

I HEADED SOUTH AFTER DRAGGING myself out the front door. For some reason I had been reluctant to go walking this morning. Once outside, I found the wind was chilly, making me wish I'd worn my red mittens. I wasn't really conscious of the houses I passed as I walked. Instead, I was in my own interior space, crowded and foggy, swimming with deep images of . . . what, I can hardly remember now.

As the oak trees came into view on my left, I looked up, wondering if the crows were waiting there again, as they had been the day before.

Sitting in the top branches, there had been about sixty of them yesterday. They would circle, land, circle, land; circling in a long massive trail of black-on-blue, melting together against the blue of the sky. *Caw, caw . . .* Deep and throaty they had called in unison. Calling for greetings or warnings I wasn't sure, but I had stood there for ten minutes or more watching their flight and listening to their voices.

"Hail, crows, you who are masters of illusion. What are you about today?"

But on this day, the day after, they were gone. Dispersed into a single apparition of their former selves, one dark spot against the sky.

Once in the park I greeted the trees, plants, and nature spirits as I always do. "Good morning, friends, blessings of a new day. What news this winter morning?"

I slowly walked the path through the forest, enjoying the crisp fresh air that hung lightly in the morning sky. I always feel at home there, loved and appreciated, knowing I can find clarity among my friends in the wild places of nature.

Coming out in the opening of a group of cork oaks, I stepped off to the right, an area that holds the energy and heart of the forest.

"Ancient Ones, thank you for holding this sacred space. Help me to find my center this day. Grant me balance and help me also to walk my life's path in humility, love, and service, for as I serve others I also serve you."

Glancing down, I noticed lying among the fallen leaves two crow claws, two crow wings, and other assorted small pieces of what was left of Crow—the leavings of Hawk's dinner yesterday, I assumed. I surveyed the sight, wondering if these remnants of Crow could be a gift for me from the Spirits of Place. Long years I have walked this nature path. Personal relationships have been formed between these spirits and myself; Crow and I had become one in knowing and purpose.

So I picked up one wing and one claw, leaving the others as my gratitude and appreciation for what had been given to me. I took them home and kept them on my altar for a few days to honor them and the spirit of the sacrifice that had been made. I now use the wing in my healing practice and keep the claw in remembrance of the power and wisdom that Crow holds.

The crows of the day before were there to tell me that indeed, balance was coming into my life, the balance I was seeking within my healing practice to help others. Crow is the keeper of sacred wisdom, and I am ever-grateful to have even a small part of that wisdom, for I hold it dear to my heart.

Victoria

Omen

In some earth-centered traditions it's considered unlucky not to greet a crow in the morning when you see one.

Crows are the caretakers of the balance between physical reality and illusion—that which cannot be readily seen with the human eye. It is Crow that can shape-shift back and forth through these realms, bringing wisdom and insight with the journey. Crow's black color signifies this ability to move undetected between the dimensions of time and space, traversing our everyday perceptions. Crow brings change, for with each thread of wisdom gained comes change. You cannot grow in a stagnant place. Crow helps you make that step toward change, bringing you wisdom found through other dimensions of reality by opening up your consciousness and building upon your knowledge. Crow wants you to look beyond what you would normally see, to expand your awareness and discover what it is that you attract into your life.

If Crow has flown your way, be prepared to gain something, some bits of wisdom, some form of inner vision or something you have been longing to understand. Crow is bringing you a message from the Otherworld.

DEER

After visiting the park near my house for a number of years, I had found it was unusual to see deer there. Once in a while I had come upon them, but they were few and far between. This day took a different turn.

I had gone to the movies the night before to see *What the Bleep Do We Know!?* I was interested in Dr. Joe Dispenza's remarks about asking for a sign from Spirit—a sign acknowledging that he'd been heard in his quest to create his day. I thought I'd try it out. I talk with Spirit all the time but had never considered asking for a sign that I'd been heard; I always knew that I was. But this morning I decided to do just that: ask for a sign I would not normally see, and one that would make me smile.

Making my familiar rounds in the park, picking up trash and communing with the spirits of nature as I went,

I headed for my special place where I talk with the Lady I serve and leave an offering. At that place, a canopy of trees hangs over the path, one fallen branch angled so low you have to stoop to get under it. Bending low, I ducked the branch so as not to hit my head—you can't see a thing in the process—then stood up. There in front of me was a beautiful six-point buck, looking as shocked to see me as I was to see him.

We stood there watching each other and wondering if we should make a dash for it. The buck didn't move, so I started talking to him, saying all was well and I wouldn't harm him, I had just come to make an offering and have a chat. He seemed okay with this, for he slowly took about four steps away and started grazing on the grass underfoot. Then I heard a noise to my right—another buck, four points. I hadn't moved yet, so I suppose he agreed I was okay and started grazing like the first buck. As I slowly started making my way toward my offering place, the deer slowly made their way away from me, grazing as they went, until they disappeared into the brush. I did what I went there to do, then started back in a different direction up the path for home.

As I went through the oak trees I saw the deer again beside the path, so I stopped and watched them. They had locked antlers in a push-pull rutting game. I had never seen real deer in a real setting doing what real deer do, exercising their instincts, being deer. It was fascinating and entertaining to see. Clearly they were enjoying themselves. This wasn't a serious matter; this was play and practice.

As I stood watching, I gave my thanks for the sign I had asked for. It reaffirmed to me that we are always heard, no matter where we are on life's path, whether we ask for a sign or not. Sometimes, though, it is just nice to see a physical manifestation of it, for that one truly did make me smile.

Victoria

Omen

Deer teaches us about gentleness and caring. It is one of the animals most often used as a helper and guide in shamanic work because its energy-force matches a human's.

Deer is about listening from the heart with patience and love, being who you innately are and not putting on airs or letting the ego get out of hand, and not forcing your views and opinions on others who might see things differently.

If Deer has come to you, look for the gentle, nurturing part of your spirit that needs to be shared. By sending out kindness and love, that kindness and love will come back to you threefold.

DOG

IT WAS LABOR DAY WEEKEND, the last hurrah of summer, and I was hurriedly packing my bags to go out of town. Normally I didn't take along my red Afghan hound, Khalamir, but there was no one to watch her this weekend: everyone else had the same idea, getting out of town. So she was coming with me.

Khalamir was a dog with an unusually calm and quiet temperament. She hardly ever got upset, and when she did she was never known to bark or bite. True to her bloodline, she was always regal in her demeanor.

Packing, I heard a knock at the door and went to see who it was. I opened it and, looking out through the screen door, found a boy of about eight peering back at me with a smile on his face. He asked if he could mow my lawn, because his mom's birthday was in two days and he needed to earn some extra money so he could buy her a present.

The moment I had opened the door, Khalamir had both paws flush up against the door frame, growling and barking at the boy in a way I had never heard before. I locked the screen to keep her from pushing through. She was adamant; she was definitely trying to tell me something.

I tried to quiet her, pushing her back into the house as I went out to give the boy five dollars and show him where the lawnmower was kept. Then I grabbed my bags and my dog, locked the doors to the house, and climbed into the car, waving goodbye to the boy as I backed out of the driveway.

Khalamir was agitated for the first part of the weekend, pacing back and forth in the cabin, barking at any little noise she heard. It was totally unlike her, and I couldn't figure out what the problem was. I was really starting to worry, but she eventually calmed down.

The rest of the weekend flew by, and that Monday evening we headed for home. As I pulled into the driveway and stopped the car, Khalamir started barking again. When I opened the door, she bounded over me like a flash. I got out myself and hurriedly unlocked the front door, because I could hear the phone ringing behind it. Khalamir just stood outside barking.

As I talked on the phone, I started to look around the living room. Things were missing—big things. I had been robbed.

I hung up and considered my options. Deciding it wasn't a good idea to be in the house alone, I went outside, grabbed my dog, and headed off to my neighbors' to use their telephone. I called a sheriff friend of mine and asked him what I should do. He came right over, and we took a short inventory of what was missing. He advised me not to stay there that night, so I called some other friends and went to their home instead. Khalamir didn't calm down until their house came into view.

The next day I went home, made a more precise list of what was missing, and turned it over to the Sheriff's Department.

A week later as I was driving to work, I noticed a yard sale going on at one of the houses on the street. Driving past the house, I was shocked to see that most of the items in the sale were mine. There were my stolen items, displayed smack in the middle of someone else's yard. I couldn't believe it. I pulled over and stared out the window, saying to myself, *That's my stuff!*

I eventually regained my composure, drove on to work, and called my sheriff friend again to tell him what was happening. Together we drove back to the yard sale and confronted the owners about what I had discovered. The boy who had mowed my lawn lived there, and it turned out that these people had perpetual yard sales of other peoples' stolen property. The kids would find the items to steal, then the parents went to collect. I don't know why they thought they'd never get caught. But that day they got caught with their hands in the proverbial cookie jar.

And Khalamir, such a smart girl, had tried to let me know in advance what was going to happen—but I hadn't understood. Who says animals don't have a sixth sense? I know from first-hand experience that they do.

Kathy

Omen

In ancient lore, dogs were considered guardians of paths and roadways. Symbolically they were seen as guarding the threshold between the land of the living and the traditional lands of the departed. Dog was there to make sure everyone found their way safely. We need not fear when he's around.

Dogs are faithful guardians and protectors of humanity. They serve out of love and loyalty to those they are entrusted to, and they never ask for anything in return.

Dog will watch over what is his and warn of coming dangers. He never hesitates to protect, even if it means sacrificing himself to do so. Dog shows us what friendship and devotion can be. He also shows us the true nature of honor and duty. If you follow Dog's example on your own path through life, you will have honored his.

Strive to give service and love to others in the tradition of Dog, and he will always walk by your side and show you the way.

DRAGON

FEET FLAT ON THE FLOOR, slow, even breaths, eyes closed. With music playing in the background, I opened my inner vision and saw only blackness—until out of the shadows appeared a dragon's head. His eyes were directly in front of mine, the scales of his head shining black, silver, purple, and gray, in shimmering waves of color. Piercing black eyes stared intently for a few moments, and then he was gone.

A brief pause—and then we were gliding high above the clouds, melting into a single being, the dragon and I becoming one. Soaring above the mass of vapors suspended in the sky, I could feel the power of my wings as each stroke rolled from my shoulders to my wing tips, carrying me up and maintaining my flight with slow, steady, languid yet powerful ease.

As I descended back toward the earth, the clouds opened, revealing dark green meadows, gently rolling hills, lush forests, and clear blue lakes fed by rushing streams. I glided above the landscape and a group of dwellings beside a distant lake came into view. I gathered my energies, ready to aim a fiery blast of destruction at the village below. I did not want to cause so much damage, but I surrendered myself to the dragon and the duty we must perform. As I swooped to treetop level, the edge of the village lay before me. I let loose a firestorm upon the thatched-roof houses below, setting them ablaze. Screaming in fear and hatred, the people rushed from their burning homes casting rocks, spears, and arrows skyward—which fell short of their target as I flew off.

I soon reached the tops of the clouds and was once again transformed, this time into a raven. Gliding on the warm air currents I flew many miles until dark, my eyes intently focused on the horizon.

In the distant desert wilderness I was drawn to a fire burning bright and hot as it lit up the night sky. It beckoned me, and so I went. Landing by the fire, I then took the form of a dancing man. A bird headdress and a cloak shaped like black wings had formed around my body. I moved sun-wise around the fire, raising and lowering my arms and stamping my feet to the rhythm of flight—a solitary shape moving through the night.

I stamped the circle around the fire again and again, then rose straight up and became a blood-red dragon, eyes to the stars, wings outstretched, tail straight behind. I began my spiraling ascent, trailing a shower of dark red sparks in my wake—a comet of pure red energy, flying into the infinite as the music slowed and my journey ended.

Dave

Omen

Dragons are mythical creatures and keepers of lakes, rivers, and caves. In many legends, they have underground lairs where they guard treasure and ancient esoteric wisdom from those unprepared or unworthy to be entrusted with such gifts. Caves, the inner recesses of the earth, connect dragons with the primal forces of nature, and with our own innermost selves.

The word *dragon* is derived from the Latin *draco* or *draconis,* which means "snake" or "serpent" but can also mean "sight." Dragons are associated with wisdom, leadership, strength, mastery, longevity, and initiation.

In Wales, the national flag has a red dragon emblem, alluding to the legends of Merlin, who prophesied of a great battle between two dragons—one red, one white. The red dragon referred to the Britons, who are today represented by the Welsh. The white dragon represented the Saxons, who invaded Britain in the fifth and sixth centuries. The red dragon prevailed and is honored on the Welsh flag. This tale is featured in the Welsh manuscript *The Mabinogion*, a collection of prose stories.

In the astrological Chinese horoscope, Dragon is the fifth sign of twelve and is considered a bringer of good luck, a benevolent but powerful being. Dragons only started to be perceived as evil, fearsome beasts in medieval Europe. Previously they had been revered as the strength and power of the land, representing supreme authority to rule.

Dragon, as well as Snake, also depicts our own inner fire or Kundalini. It remains coiled at the base of the spine until we are emotionally prepared for it to rise up through our energy centers, or chakras, opening us to deeper wisdom and subtle communion with the Divine. Care is needed to not wake the dragon before its time, for power and deep spiritual knowledge are only truly benevolent when we have gained a degree of self-mastery and balance. Before that time, we are indeed toying with fire.

There are four dragons, which also represent the four elements of air, earth, fire, and water. The message you receive depends on which dragon comes to you. Look at each elemental sign, search out its meaning, apply it to your circumstance, and then ask. Remain open for the message to appear. You will always get an answer. It may appear in a dream, or it may appear symbolically through nature. You may read something that pertains to it, or the answer may come through a television program you happen to watch. But when it does come, it will be crystal clear; there won't be any doubt—and confirmation will come from your higher self. Patience is always a key to gaining information. Cultivate patience by living it.

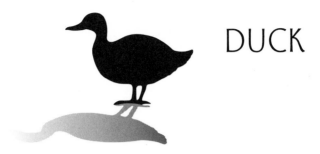

DUCK

"IT ISN'T RIGHT. I THINK we should be born old, then grow young, provided we could hang on to our wisdom. Someone got it backward."

I was talking to Balthazar. He had eased in through the trees as I sat with my back against a cypress. Nine of them stood staggered from my vantage point on the ground. I knew this was an illusion, though, for when you stepped onto the path you could see they were all lined up in straight rows of seven across and forty-two deep.

"What's wrong?" Balthazar asked. "Feeling the pull of another birthday?" He smiled.

"It's only a month away. Do you realize that I'll be the same age as the last two digits of my birth year? I'm pushing middle age and I don't care for it!" Only one other birthday had really bothered me before. It was an obscure number that shouldn't have mattered at all, but it had. Now here I was with the same number on the end again—three. What was there about threes?

I had come into the woods to think. This age thing was interesting in its own right, but at the moment I wasn't finding it particularly so.

Balthazar was now sitting across from me on a fallen cypress, blue eyes sparkling and hair black as a raven's wing.

"Little Sister, why do you fret so? Not much has changed since last we were together in physical form. You worried overmuch even back then. I thought I had taught you better."

He had made his presence known to me one night around a celebratory fire honoring Lughnasadh. He had come to help me lighten up. It was true, I always seemed to take things more seriously than they needed to be taken. He had come into my life in a humorous way, causing good-natured mischief. Now I had come to rely on his gentle guidance and understanding of life, plus his ideas about fun.

"I guess it just appears that my life is getting away from me. There's so much more I want to do." Turning my head, I looked toward the edge of the northern bank of trees, hoping he hadn't noticed the quiver in my voice as I tried to choke down my emotions.

"Age is irrelevant in the whole scheme of things. Age is something that happens to the body to prepare it for shifting dimensions and move the spirit toward evolution. There is no age of the spirit. You of all people should know that." He looked at me so intently that I felt myself start to squirm, then he continued.

"Spirit is timeless. It's not something that can be measured in days, or years, or even millennia. It doesn't move along a long extended line. It's not linear—it's more cyclical, if you need to put a simple picture to it. It's a mistaken concept that it can be calculated."

He was right, of course, but at the moment it wasn't something I wanted to hear, so instead of acknowledging that fact, I stood up. "I need to walk," I murmured, turning toward the path. Out of the corner of my eye I saw him smile at me, then walk through the underbrush around the grove and slip out of sight beyond the oaks.

Good, I thought. I wanted to wallow in my self-pity, and he never allowed me to do that.

Surprisingly, I found myself alone on the road that had merged with the pathway. As I rolled my conversation with Balthazar around in my mind, my walking picked up speed.

"What are you creating?" he had asked. "A new view of what age can be? Or are you giving in to the stereotypical? The force that holds you in this space is negativity. Will you give yourself over to it? For the energy that you place into it is the energy you'll get in return."

I knew that this kind of negative energy usually collapses in on you. I needed a way to turn my thinking around and pull myself out of it, so I headed for the creek where I always went when I was having issues with my emotions.

I moved down the bank and knelt by the creekside, watching it drift along, a swaying stream of crystal blue water. As I gazed in, I felt myself start to relax, my self-imposed stress flowing down into the earth below my feet, washed away as I was purified by her gentle energies.

"My Lady, I've come seeking your counsel." I closed my eyes, and with that my supplication began.

Consummate union takes me past the boundaries of time or space into my center where she dwells in perfect trust and perfect love. Seeping into every pore of this fleshy body like a brilliant shaft of light pours through cloud cover. She is ever-present in my life, but never more so than when we are in communion together. And it flows.

Slowly I pulled back to myself and sensed Balthazar to my right. I opened my eyes. He stood leaning against a sycamore tree that had rooted next to the creek, gazing out as if in thought.

"Look." He nodded his head toward the creek. "There's your number three again."

I found three ducks floating with the current. It pushed them downstream; they paddled back. Down, back, staying close to where we stood watching.

Two were all white with black backs and upper wings, dark greenish-black heads, and scarlet beaks. The other had mottled gray feathers with a reddish-chestnut head. Beautiful. White, red, black. Maiden, Mother, Crone. The Goddess is ever present.

"Did you know this?" I asked.

He just shrugged his shoulders as if to say, "Do you doubt?"

I didn't. For I knew that some lessons are best learned on the inner plane, and some manifest on the physical.

"I believe there's a message here for you. If you're willing to see it." Leaning down, he picked up a rock at his feet and held it in his hand, studying it intently.

I knew what he meant. If I was willing to accept what was being offered, beyond what my eyes saw. "Okay," I conceded. "You win."

A big smile lit his eyes, shining from the inner fire that he holds. "I wasn't trying to win. I just know how obstinate you can be at times. I always have to come in through the back door when you're in that space and I want to teach you something. Now admit it, would you have been receptive?"

He was right: I wouldn't have. I had wanted to fall into that place where I hold myself in emotional bondage. I don't like it there, but it is familiar. I nurture it like mother with child.

We sat for a time watching the ducks. They were happily taking their leisure close to the bank's edge. I looked over at Balthazar and there was that smile again, a smile that could always melt an ice cube buried in snowcaps.

"You want me to tell you what kind they are?"

I sighed. "No. I'll find that out on my own, thanks."

And so later that day I did. The ducks were a breed that was totally new to me, Common Mergansers. My negativity had taken a turn and disappeared, for the ducks had helped me connect with the energies of water. I had received a healing through the Mergansers and guidance through Balthazar. I was grateful to both.

Victoria

Omen

In the natural world, ducks are considered waterfowl. And on a metaphysical level, ducks are associated with humans' emotional nature because they are so closely connected to water. When we attune ourselves to water and water elements, our moods can be changed, negativity and low emotional energy can be altered, and healing can begin.

With Duck's connection to water and the emotional plane, we can gain knowledge and skill pertaining to creativity, compassion, love, healing, tranquility, and all right-brain functions. And this can help us become emotionally balanced in the process of becoming self-actualized, a state we are all moving toward.

By working with Duck and the associated element of water, you can create positive emotional outlooks, empower your sense of compassion, and promote a serene, peaceful attitude.

As an omen, Duck asks, How you are moving through life? Do you move along smooth and easily, or do you stubbornly fight what comes? Do you embrace changes, or do you wrestle them for control? Do you try to prevent emotional pain by blocking your feelings so you don't have to deal with them—and then get stuck in an unhealthy situation or mind-set?

Don't create obstacles by holding on to views that bring about disharmony. Instead, promote healing by calling your energies back to you from the rigid emotional bindings you have placed around them. Rely on Duck's tranquil example and guidance, and on the inner strength you have gained thus far.

EGRET

IT WAS ANOTHER OF THOSE socked-in foggy days we usually get around here in January. Two weeks straight and we were all getting pretty tired of it.

My father had come to visit because I wanted to take him to my special place in the park. I had found a rare occurrence manifested there, and he wanted to see it for himself. He's always open to the unusual. I don't take just anyone to my special place, for it is my nemeton, my temple. But this day was different, and my father is deeply intuitive, so I wanted to share with him what I had found.

Our conversation ran along spiritual lines: energy, trees, our place in and understanding of life on this earthly plane.

When we got back from our adventure we sat for an hour or so at the dining table, discussing reincarnation. The time went by in a warm and happy way, as it always does when I'm with my dad. When he got up to leave, I followed him outside onto the front porch. As I stood telling him goodbye he motioned for me to *look there*.

On the peak of the roof of my neighbors' house, not more than fifty feet away, was a beautiful white egret, looking quite out of place. I stood transfixed by what I was seeing. Egrets don't usually wander far from marshes or swamps, so it's quite unusual to see one on the roof of a house within the city limits. As I was grasping the oddity of the situation, the egret spread her wings and flew off in an easterly direction. I thought, *Now there's an omen if I ever saw one.*

Victoria

Omen

The egret is a medium-sized, all-white heron. Its habitats are marshes, ponds, swamps, and mud flats. Egrets and bitterns belong to the same family of birds—a family that does not include cranes, although cranes do resemble herons.

The egret often feeds by reaching one foot forward in the water where it stands, rapidly vibrating it to scare up prey. Then, lightning fast, it catches the fish and insects swimming by.

Herons and cranes were said to be the first to face the rising sun, and so were associated with the element of fire and the east, the direction of spiritual knowledge and hidden secrets.

Egrets are exceptional examples of balance, patience, and the ability to bring focus and direction to bear on a goal or purpose.

If Egret has flown into your life, check to see if a condition or situation has recently manifested—one that perhaps you have been blind to, and are just now fully realizing. Maybe this situation could best be served by your thinking it through first, then *acting* on your best judgment, rather than *reacting* emotionally to it. On the other hand, maybe you are overanalyzing the situation and instead need to trust your intuition.

When we are not united or balanced in our thinking, life can become a never-ending circle of confusion. Egret's power to move with surety and decisiveness is the example to follow. Egret will lead us to understand what to do and how to move forward with confidence, knowing we can deal rationally with any uncertainty that comes into our lives and gain a sense of clarity and stability.

FOX

THE MINUTE MY FEET HIT the ground I knew this place was special, even if the old red tool shed with the broken-out windows wasn't in the best of shape and the house left a lot to be desired.

The land, though—the land sang its own sacred song. I could feel this song lingering around the soles of my shoes as I stood looking up to the summit of Castle Rock rising high above this property. The land's energy curled around my toes, then moved higher into my calves as it pushed against my bones, melted into muscle and flesh, then filled my head with cool splashes of sound that raced out through the top of my brow as it caught and mingled with the breeze. It left me feeling vibrantly alive and connected with the land where I stood.

I was searching for a new home, a new place to lay down roots. And even though I had felt the life and pull of this place instantly, I wasn't quite convinced. The house had been vacant for six months. I could have pushed my finger through the windowsills, they were so rotten. The house was built on an old creek bed, which meant a lot of extra muscle and time if I wanted to have a garden or do any landscaping. It made me pause and think.

But a creek flowing thirty-five feet from the house was very appealing. I could sit outside at twilight listening to the sounds of a creek inundated with the harmonious melody of frogs, and the eerie night cries of the owls flying down from their perching places among the cover of trees to hunt along the creek. The water would pay tribute to the mystery and darkness of the night in choruses heard only by those blessed to be out and present. Yes, it was very appealing.

The realtor and I wandered around discussing options, then he suggested I stay for a while to think about it. He drove off, and I headed down to the creek. I stepped into the water to survey what needed to be done to shore up the bank and keep it running along its original winding passageway. I picked up a rock and hefted it off to the side where it could buttress the bank. Then I hefted another, and another. The place wasn't mine yet, but working here on the creek seemed the thing to do at that moment. It helped me think, physical and mental powers perfectly in sync.

As I moved the rocks left and right, I had a sudden feeling I was being watched. It took a minute for this to register mentally, then I looked up. At the top of the embankment, watching me with profound interest, was a red fox. Our eyes met and he seemed to ask the question, *What are you doing there in the water of my neighborhood, hey?* And then he was gone just as quickly as he had appeared, headed toward the tangle of blackberry bushes. Part of me felt accepted; part of me was left to wonder.

Later that day I ventured out to an estate sale put on by some friends in town, leaving my indecision about the property spinning around in my brain.

Rummaging through a box of knick-knacks and cast-off items at the sale, I stumbled upon an old bronze door-knocker shaped like a fox. At that moment clarity came to me; the decision was made. The fox on the bank, the fox in the box of goods—could an answer have been clearer? I purchased the doorknocker, then went home to make the deal with the realtor.

The red fox and I have since agreed to share the space. At first I saw him on a regular basis whenever I was in the creek, then for a while he was gone. But he's back now, along with others of his kind, freely inhabiting the property

I now hold in trust for those who walked this land for generation after generation.

I can appreciate my part in all this, and the honor of being the present caretaker. As I see it, not only was the fox a sign that I should purchase the land, it was a sign that I was regarded as one of its natural inhabitants. I am grateful for the show of confidence.

John

Omen

Wily Fox, the cunning one. Fox has always been regarded as a trickster, like the Norse god Loki or the Irish god Aonghus. But Fox doesn't teach through trickery for trickery's sake. Instead, he cunningly shows us our humanity and instills in us the ability to laugh at ourselves, to lighten up and not take life so seriously.

Fox also has the ability to remain in the shadows, watching, observing what is going on around him. You may not even know you're being thus observed, but you are. If Fox makes his presence known to you, make sure you are listening, for he is offering you some information, something you need to know. He will lead you into truth and knowing, for Fox has clear vision and decisiveness.

If Fox has walked across your path, follow where he leads. He knows the ins and outs of living, he knows about the darker sides of existence, but he also knows how to live life in joy. As he laughs at himself, he is trying to teach you how to integrate that humor into your own life. *Lighten up,* he is saying, for life passes like the ticking of a clock: one tick, one second, then that second is gone forever, never to return. So enjoy the journey, don't be distracted by the insignificant, and just be smarter than the rest.

HAWK

IN THE CITY WHERE I live, a volunteer group works with the park and recreation district to help maintain and improve the parks in the area. One of the group's jobs is to remove invasive plants from the parks—an effort that may often have mixed results, in my opinion.

One early spring morning, I found the invasive-plant people hard at work at a local park. As I made my way along the path, I heard, then spotted, two red-shouldered hawks as they called and circled overhead.

Hawk is lord of my heart—and my heart was heavy that day. Hawk teaches about balance and shows us how to release any unnecessary emotional baggage we may be carrying around. He is viewed as a messenger of the gods, so when he comes into view, be open: insight will come to you in some way.

I decided to leave the park sooner than I really wanted to because I was bothered by the group pulling the invasive plants. Was their task really necessary? In the long run, was the outcome good for all concerned, including the other plants and the animals that resided there? But as I rounded the corner, heading back for home, I heard again one hawk and then another, so I stopped and looked up, hoping to watch them for a while.

One hawk swooped over and landed in the top of an Austrian pine, then the other did the same, swooping and gliding down to meet with the first hawk settled on the branch. He did not land beside her, though, but beautifully and gently on her, and in a moment in they were locked in the throes of creation. I felt greatly privileged to be witness to such a beautiful sight. And how apropos, for right under the tree where they had landed were the invasive-plant people, who were ending life, while up above them life was being created.

The great circle: birth, life, death, rebirth. Around and around it goes, never permanently ending, always beginning. It made me take another look at the plant-pullers and their task. I didn't necessarily agree with it, but the awareness of the great circle helped me release any judgments about why they do it.

The whole situation—the plants, the hawks, and my heavy heart—reminded me of that circular reality. Things are always in motion. While one thing happens above, another quite opposite thing happens below. Change comes to all existence; in the scheme of things it is inevitable. Some changes are voluntary and some are forced upon us, but all are presented to help us learn, grow, and evolve. It was being conveyed the way nature intended. The measure of my understanding was limited only by my inability to see clearly. Release that which no longer serves, and don't cling to outmoded aspects of your life.

I certainly got the message that day and am grateful to those who sent it.

Victoria

Omen

Hawks are beautiful, stately birds of prey. They move us on a deep primal level: the way they sail with their wings set against the pull of the wind, their characteristic call from far within the woods. How could there be any doubt about their place among the gods—as messengers come from beyond the north wind?

Hawks are equipped to bring knowledge and insight to the earthly inhabitants. As visionaries from higher realms, they teach us to observe what is going on around us that we might be missing, what piece of life's puzzle could help us see our way more clearly.

Do you feel "off," not yourself in some sense? Are your trials weighing you down or causing you to feel out of balance? Hawk may come to help you see where you can find your center again. Stop and listen to that still, soft voice from the Otherworldly realm: it is admonishing you to reclaim your power, including your power of discernment, for this discernment offers clues on how to proceed on our life path with the vision of Hawk. Rise above that which hinders and fly higher to your true self, knowing that what had been obscured can now be seen and released.

HORSE

ONE SUMMER IN THE 1970S, my wife, Judy, her son, Jon, and I decided to go camping in the northern Nevada desert. A year earlier, my friend Paul and I had enjoyed camping at Spring Creek in that area. Judy and I were just starting our life together, so I wanted to share with her this special place.

Near Spring Creek is an old mining town called Midas, which has a classic rural gathering place called the Midas Bar. On that earlier trip, Paul and I had gone in for a beer and a visit with the local townsfolk. We explained that we'd been camping and knocking around northern Nevada for a few days, and we still had a few days left. The people at the bar told us if we wanted to camp at a place that was truly beautiful and seldom visited, we should four-wheel into the mountains above Midas to a valley where the Little

Humbolt River flowed through. We took their advice, and they were absolutely right. Paul and I had such a great stay that now it was the one place I wanted to be sure to take Judy and Jon.

So that summer we set out on our first camping trip together as a new family. We stayed at Spring Creek the first couple of days, fishing and exploring, then packed up camp and headed to Midas and the Little Humbolt River.

The road up the mountain was heavily rutted by the spring runoff, making the drive bumpy and slow. The air was warm and redolent with sagebrush and flower scents, and the constant buzzing of insects resonated in our ears. I looked forward to cresting the last hill that would bring us to the brink of the valley floor, for I was sure Judy and Jon would be filled with awe at the natural beauty of the place, as I had been on my first visit.

When we reached the top of the hill overlooking the valley it was as beautiful as I had remembered: a few acres of dense green grass surrounded by hills, with the Little Humbolt pouring through the far side of the valley and clumps of leafy trees scattered along the riverbed. We set up camp, eager to explore—which we did for most of that day, wandering around the valley and the hills. When we returned to camp we were hungry and ready for dinner.

While cooking, we heard the sound of galloping hooves coming our direction. Turning toward the sound, we saw a herd of wild horses crest the hill behind us and run down to the river some fifty yards downstream. Several horses bent their heads down to take a long drink from the cool water while the others stood guard. They took turns doing this, always making sure it was safe. We watched them in silence while they drank their fill, and they didn't seem the least bit disturbed by our presence. Then they turned and galloped back over the hill as quickly as they had arrived, disappearing into the desert beyond, leaving only a thin cloud of dust to mark their passing.

We stood in wonder over what we had seen. Then we took notice of the trails that surrounded the sagebrush on the hill behind our camp. These horses had made this visit many times in the past; we were just lucky enough to be there to witness it this time. That night around the camp-fire our conversation kept turning back to the horses. We wondered about, and hoped for, a return visit.

The horses did return the next evening, and each evening we were there. For a magical moment, Judy, Jon, and I were part of their lives, as they were forever to be part of ours, captured in a special memory of our trip to the valley of the Little Humbolt River.

Dave

Omen

As an omen, Horse has always been considered a power animal, able to carry its rider across landscapes of time and space to the realm between the world of humanity and the world of gods. Those seeking insight, wisdom, and healing rode horses to discover that knowledge, for Horse never faltered as a walker between these worlds.

Horse moves us along, carries our loads, and provides us with the power to achieve our goals and dreams. Horse signifies the bond between animal and rider, for Horse will ultimately carry us through to the end of our intent.

If Horse has come to you, examine your goals and see if you have the strength and determination to do what is required to achieve them. Look to Horse to help reveal the inner nature of your objective, and whether you have the skill, physical or mental, to bring it about. Horse will see that you attain your desired destination: trust in this partnership.

HUMMINGBIRD

Mid-morning, early spring, my sacred place. I'm leaning against a fallen tree that is mossed green on one side. Nearby a gray squirrel is foraging the earth for acorns and other bits of tasty squirrel food. I'm enthralled by her focus and her moments of seeming amusement when she finds her cache.

I'm so enthralled that I'm oblivious to anything else going on around me. Then I hear a sound in my left ear, the sound of swarming bees, larger-than-normal bees. I freeze, uncertain whether to turn my head and look—or should I run for it? A sting from a giant bee doesn't sound too appealing. But I decide to chance it. How many giant bees have I seen?

Slowly I turn my head. Hovering before my eyes, not more than a foot away, is the most beautiful red-breasted opalescent-green hummingbird I have ever seen. She looks at me, I look at her, understanding passes between us for a full fifteen seconds, then she's off in a flash of red-green energy. I am delighted and spellbound, for she has heard the quiet joy of my heart, the joy of being in the presence of all the Earth Mother's children.

I am filled with happiness simply being where I am. The hummer came to share her joy, for she delights in the beauty of Mother Nature as I do. We are kindred spirits and our draw to the magnificence of the Earth Mother is profound, for what the eyes drink in nourishes our soul. She sees beauty in the flowers as she helps them reproduce. I see beauty all around me in the form of trees, plants, birds, animals, and even the insects, as all contribute to maintaining life on earth.

I am blessed by the hummer's willingness to share her moment with me. Thank you, tiny faery-bird.

Victoria

Omen

Hummingbirds are quiet, amazing creatures. With their ability to fly in any direction they choose, they remind us to be flexible no matter what path we've chosen. By being flexible we can move along our life-course easier. When we are rigid in our thinking we can become hardened to the good, tending to see only the more negative aspects that life and living can hold. Rigid thoughts cause the flow of energy to slow down or cease, which then pushes us out of tune with our intuition, spirit guides, or the Divine, and our awareness to the joy of living can grow dull.

Hummingbirds are all about the joy of living. They dart here and there, experiencing life fully, happy with where they are in the eternal realm of existence.

Everyone loves Hummingbird. That's because she reminds us of what true joy and beauty can be.

If you have sighted Hummingbird, she wants you to share and spread her beauty in the world. You can help her by carrying her gift of joy with you as you go about your everyday life.

If problems need to be resolved or wrongs redressed, take Hummingbird's love with you in carrying out these tasks. If you view life not as a burden to be borne but as an opportunity to learn and grow, the joy of living will be yours, and Hummingbird will be your constant companion.

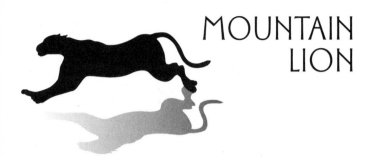

MOUNTAIN LION

I HAD SPENT THE EVENING talking with a friend at my office. He had a job that required him to be a strong leader, a role that wasn't always easy, and he had asked for my perspective on the problem.

It was near midnight when I started the drive toward home, taking the main road leading to the next town. And as I drove I felt some discomfort as my own unresolved leadership problems rattled around in my mind and body. The night was very dark and I passed no one.

I was about halfway home when up ahead I saw a large mountain lion standing in the middle of the road, watching me approach. I slowed down, then stopped the car about ten feet from where she stood motionless. We stared at each other while she held her position.

I began talking to her and felt a return energy-flow to my whole body, a communication that we kept going for at least ten minutes. Then I felt her energy pull back, and she casually strolled away.

I was grateful for the experience, feeling I had received a teaching, and I felt very calm.

Later in the month I remembered that Native Americans honor the mountain lion as the embodiment of leadership and power.

Jan

Omen

The mountain lion, or cougar, has always been linked symbolically with leadership and power.

With this role comes the responsibility to know how to use it. Those who are in leadership positions have the duty to act ethically and consider what is best for all concerned. Balance is a key issue in leadership roles—balance of power and being in a right relationship with yourself. It's easy to misuse the power of Mountain Lion for self-gain and self-advancement, so consider your own use of your role and where power truly lies.

If Mountain Lion has come into your life, examine your motives in whatever leadership role you may have. Ask yourself, "Will this help generate real change for the better for those I am leading, or will it just advance my own agenda?"

Remember that what you send out always comes back to you in the end, so make sure you exercise your ethical muscles. Strengthen your resolve to have a right relationship with yourself and others, and life will support you in your desire.

NEWT

THE PLACE IS CALLED TABLE Mountain and it's exactly what its name implies. Every year in spring it is thick with wildflowers: a sudden spread of colors pops up where none had been just days before—a display of beauty across acres of nature's dining table.

I had lived in this area all my life but had never gone to see the wildflowers of Table Mountain, although my friend had talked about it more than once. On this day the subject came up again, so we decided this was it, this was our chance. We hopped in his car and took off.

It was still early spring and the rains hadn't slacked off much. The ground was wet when we arrived at the parking lot near the trailhead, but the sun was out, filling me with a sweet warmth that flowed like honey down my spine.

The path lay ahead, across what looked like a moderately damp area. But our attempt at a direct crossing failed: soon water was running over the tops of my shoes. After mucking through, wondering if I would lose my cross-trainers in the mud, we found our way to the path. Now mind you, that wasn't too hard because the only trees in sight, except for a few scrub oaks dotting the landscape, were five or six Valley Oaks congregating along the stream that paralleled the path.

This congregation of oaks had picked a great spot because it was green and meadowy. The stream was a bit wider here, and the grass grew tall in the shade of the oaks. Here and there a cow meandered along, chewing the tender stalks and looking up periodically as someone wandered by.

I stopped and left an offering among the oaks. The presence of Spirit was palpable in that lovely place, and I was drawn to give my thanks for the beauty and enjoyment it gave.

We continued along the path that wandered next to the stream, eventually coming to an area where the water cascaded over the side of a cliff into a pool. People were at the bottom splashing and wading, but it was too steep for me to climb, so instead we made our way along the top of the rim and over a small hill.

There it was—a little pool of water caught between a small rise in the land and the hill we had just crossed. It wasn't more than four feet across, but it looked fresh. We needed to sit down, so down we went along the edge.

My friend saw him first: a little newt under the water at the far end, sitting on the bottom in the shade of a rock. He was lovely, brown with a burnt-orange underbelly and little splayed-out toes half-embedded in the mud. I wanted to get a better look, so I asked him if he would come closer, over *here*—and I pointed to a spot right in front of me. This he did, slowly making his way toward us, stopping now and again. He came to rest in the exact spot I had asked, then swam up to the surface of the water, took a gulp of air, and swam back down to lounge again on the bottom of the pool.

I'm not sure how long we sat watching him. It must have been twenty minutes or more. The world around us was dead silent except for an occasional bird calling and a slight breeze whistling over our heads. I felt myself getting sleepy and wondered whether something other than the sun on my back was casting its spell. It's a known fact that when the Sidhe are around, the Old Irish gods, you can be lulled to sleep for long periods if you're not careful. Look at Rip Van Winkle—a fairy tale? Maybe.

The sun was dropping lower in the sky, so we decided it was better to head home instead of getting caught after dark with no lights to guide us. I left an offering to the Spirits of Place and the newt in thanks for a lovely experience and a beautiful day.

That wasn't the end of it, though. Over the next three nights I slept more deeply and peacefully than I had since childhood. I took several extended naps, two to three hours each. And my sense of time was totally off. The morning after our walk, the clock in my bedroom had stopped, and after I reset it, I found that it was fifteen minutes fast when I glanced at it hours later. The next day, I ended up forty-five minutes late for an appointment when my wristwatch stopped after I had set it to remind me.

During those three days I thought again and again of my experience with the newt. I felt literally giddy whenever I thought about it, and I had a profound longing to go back there, an almost overwhelming desire.

Finally I figured I'd better get a grip on the situation.

I had learned that in the natural places where the Sidhe are known to dwell, enchantment is more prevalent than elsewhere. To enchant means to charm, or to fill with song, and there had been a lot of song that day: the trickle of the stream, the whistle of the wind, the melody of the birds, the rustle of grass. It just depends on what your view of song is.

So I took out my garnet locket and put it on. Garnets help strengthen the aura, ground the spirit and offer protection. I wore it for the next week and finally started feeling better and more like myself.

I never forgot the little newt, though, or my experience at Table Mountain. I still plan to go back there in the future. Only this time I'm going to wear my locket.

Victoria

Omen

Newts are amphibians and spend their lives partly in water and partly on land. They are cold-blooded, drawing on the surrounding environment for warmth. Amphibians molt their skin and can regenerate body parts that are injured or lost. They have strong homing instincts and are said to use the sun or moon as clues for direction.

As an omen, Newt teaches us never to take anything for granted. What we see with our eyes can be entirely different from what really is. Newt also teaches about transformation, how we can take our ideas and turn them into solid form, watching for the assured signs of growth in these areas.

Newt shows us that home is never far away because we always carry an aspect of home in our hearts wherever we go. We can find our way back to the source, our spiritual home, if we just look inward and trust Spirit to guide us.

If Newt has come to you, prepare for new developments or growth to happen in your life. Have you been longing for a new path to follow, or a new outlook? Then Newt has come to help you actualize these into being. Accept yourself as whole right now, but let Newt open doors to newness and possibility. Put one foot forward and go.

OSPREY

My fishing lure just floated on top of the water. It hadn't made a ripple for hours. Across the blue two-acre pond I could see an osprey sitting high on a limb hanging over the water's edge. She seemed to be watching—what, I wasn't sure, but I felt exposed just thinking I might be what she was looking at. To an observer, it's obvious if the fish are biting. A top-water lure tells no lies. It will bob under even on the smallest nibbles, so you can see why I felt a sense of vulnerability. Not getting a bite for hours, even on a recreational outing, is quite an insult to a fisherman.

As I was getting ready to give up and go home, the osprey spread out her wings and stepped off the branch. Down she glided, closer and closer to the glassy smooth reflection of her image on the water-top.

Splash. I saw her talons penetrate the water, bringing up a glittering silver fish. She soared toward me, fish in tow, and circled twice over my head. I got the distinct impression that those circles were her way of saying, "This is how you catch a fish!"

Then she flew back to perch on the branch where she had started. There she sat, taking the fish apart with her beak in a delicate and precise manner.

Well, she didn't need to prove to me that day how inferior a pole and line were: she ended up with a tasty morsel, and I went home empty-handed. In the long run I had to concede that her way of fishing was better, but that wouldn't keep me from trying my hand at it again. I may not have wings or the gift of flight, but I do have determination and hope.

Dan

Omen

Ospreys are gifted water birds and hunters, and their diets are almost exclusively fish. When hunting they dive feet first for their prey, as eagles do. But unlike eagles, ospreys may deliberately dive underwater, completely submerging themselves as they tug their prey to the surface.

Ospreys are sometimes mistaken for eagles because of their all-white heads and their similar nests—large heaps of sticks atop cliff outcrops, tall trees, telephone poles, and bridges. But this diving ability is unique to the osprey.

And it gives the osprey the power, as an omen animal, to look below and beyond the surface of the physical world. The osprey brings us insight and knowledge, showing how to look inside for our own true destiny, for who and what we are on a deeper level.

On a metaphysical level, ospreys also signify cleansing or purification because of their ability to immerse themselves in water. In doing so, they demonstrate how to get rid of stagnant energy and replace it with fresh. Osprey may show us when a cleansing in some form needs to be undertaken in our life. Have we come to the time to turn away from the things that hold us back, whether it is someone, something, or a certain state of mind? Osprey can help tame our fears, cleanse our thinking, and reveal our truths. So pay attention, we are being told: look inside for what you seek. Your destiny is reflected there.

OWL

I CONSIDERED IT A GOOD omen to see an owl on the first morning of the new year. Most owls are nocturnal, so seeing one during the day is an out-of-the-ordinary experience. Plus, it was a brand new year.

I had intended to go for my walk early that morning. Three days had passed and the trees were calling me. But as I looked out my window I saw that the rain clouds were finally releasing their pent-up moisture. The wind was blowing from the cold northern sky, sending large drops angling sideways toward the ground and leaving puddles strewn about the yard.

Damn, I thought, and gave up the idea. But just as quickly I took hold of it again, grabbed my hat and walking stick, then headed for the door. I wasn't going to let the wet weather keep me away.

Walking my usual path toward the park, I decided at the last minute to take the left-fork detour through the mud and leaves heavy with rain. I could find the high places through this passage; I had been this way before. When I reached the area I was headed for, I slid ever so quietly into the redwood's circular branch canopy.

As I did, I caught sight of two wings above me as they beat out a whoosh of air through white-beige feathers. An owl had stepped from the branch and out into flight. It was the one and only sound I heard from her. Up she flew, like prayers rising on smoke, the energy left behind thick and cohesive, mingling with mine. I closed my eyes and drank it in, feeling the Nature Spirits nodding their approval.

My guides called to me from the cover of trees, reminding me of the freedom I share to soar toward the sky like the owl, if I could just let go of what keeps me bound to the earth. It wasn't to be that day, though—my conscious thoughts brought me back down.

I pulled the sage and lavender from my pocket and offered it to the four directions, Spirits of Place, and the Lady I serve.

"Happy New Year. Blessings of a brand-new morning and another day in which to manifest peace, happiness, and healing." I left the offering in the center of the tree circle along with my prayers of thanks.

It was a good way to start the new year and a good omen besides.

Victoria

Omen

Owls, being primarily nocturnal, have come to represent mystery and magic because of their connection to the night. Silent flight is their advantage in hunting and also in living undetected in the world. This ability to live in the dark, to see through darkness and discern the subtleties that abound there, also represents Owl's connection to the Dark Goddess, the Crone, the Hag of the Hills. It is she who travels in this darkness to bring wisdom and insight into the lives of the seeker, for she sees what others can't or choose not to see.

Owl brings with her ancient knowledge, for she is one of the oldest of the old. She teaches us what was, what is, and what is to come, imparting the ability to know our past, present, and future with clarity. As one of the ancient ones, Owl stands apart for her skill in foreseeing in all directions; she can bring her knowledge silently forward into the light of day.

If Owl has come, it could be the time to study the Diviner's Art, to bring knowledge and soul-level information to those who are seeking it, including yourself. By helping others look into all areas of existence, you can assist them in discovering that answers can be found; it is a matter of letting oneself see and remain open to them.

Exploring the mysteries can bring great understanding. It can encourage us to listen to our natural intuition by expanding outside our normal perceptions of reality. All that is waits to be discovered.

RABBIT

THE SUN WAS RISING BEYOND a distant hill, and as I stood taking in the view it crested the summit, flooding light into the morning sky, one beam stabbing the earth between two great stones near my feet. I stood frozen in the stones' shadow, caught breathless by the force of the light pulling at the sky, changing its color from cobalt to azure blue.

A rustling of scotch broom startled me out of my daze. Out of the underbrush two large brown ears emerged, then a furry black body—a cottontail rabbit. Then I noticed, to my surprise, that a spotted fawn was standing nearby in the shadows. I didn't move except to breathe. The rabbit hopped right up to the fawn and took great care to settle itself at the fawn's feet. Then the fawn shifted its position a bit, and so did the rabbit. Then again, practically in unison: whenever

85

the fawn took a step, so did the rabbit. They moved in perfect harmony, like well-rehearsed partners in a dance.

I found this fascinating. An obvious bond was there, but what kind of bond? Was the rabbit seeking safety and felt comfortable in the fawn's company? It was a mystery, and a mystery it remained, for I soon resumed my walk down the hill along the path of light that had greeted me at sunup.

It wasn't until I got home and related the story to my daughter that I understood the connection with the rabbit.

I had awoken that morning with worry on my mind. The future of a loved one had been causing me concern, and my sleep had been restless. It was not really my place to take on this worry, but I do tend to dwell on anxieties this way.

From what I was told, rabbits are linked to fears. Apparently I needed to see that my fear and worry were really self-inflicted, and it would be wise to release them. I guess the rabbit had a message for me other than what I could see visually. It was a learning experience, and I'll try to remember to stay open, so these kinds of messages can come through.

Howard

Omen

Rabbits and hares have been linked with the faery realm, moon deities, and moon magic. They symbolize fertility, birth, transformation, and healing.

Rabbit's feet are traditionally carried for good luck, and it's believed that rubbing one can make your dreams and wishes come true. Hares are bearers of good fortune and have been used as divinatory animals. Rabbits, on the other hand, can be connected with fears and anxiety. Being timid creatures, they are easy prey for other larger animals.

If Rabbit has hopped your way, ask to see the bigger picture behind your agitation or anxiety. Are these real dangers or presumed dangers born out of fear? If they are fear-based, where is this feeling generated from? Does it come from your head or is it centered in your stomach? Correct signals, carrying pertinent information, usually come through your heart center, or heart chakra.

Sometimes our own fears can bring pain into being. So search out where your fear is based, and then listen to the voice of your higher self. It will direct you in seeking out healing, then transformation will follow.

SEAL

THE SKY WAS ROBIN'S-EGG BLUE and the sun was hazy and warm the morning I went to the beach. The weather was still cool enough for a coat, though, as it always is on the Northern California coast. I had gone there by myself to think and enjoy the sound of the waves and the smell of the salt air. The beach was deserted, which is the way I always prefer it. I like the time alone to commune with whichever spirits may be around.

While walking and looking for seashells I caught a glimpse of something about twenty feet offshore, something bobbing up and down with the waves. At first I didn't take much notice, being distracted by my shell search. But when I looked up again I started paying more attention, for the shape was still there, having moved along with me down the beach.

My first thought was that it was a cluster of seaweed bulbs floating along with the tide. But when one bulb grew a snub nose with whiskers on each side, and the green seaweed color turned to gray, I knew my first impression had been wrong. No seaweed here: instead I found two dark curious eyes looking at me over the water's edge, a harbor seal swimming and floating along, mingling with the foamy kelp that is the hiding place for its dinner.

This was pretty exciting; I had never seen a seal this close to shore or along this inlet of beach. I stopped and looked at her for a while, and she floated and looked back at me. Then, as I continued down the beach, I noticed the seal kept up with me on her watery path, keeping pace with my own starts and stops on my shell watch. She disappeared periodically, only to reappear right opposite me, making eye contact whenever she rose up from the sea. She followed me all the way down to where the cliffs meet the sand and you can go no farther, then she turned as I turned to walk back up the beach toward camp.

That's when I started to marvel at the rarity of this experience. How many harbor seals will follow a human up and down a beach a third of a mile long? Is this little gray-furred thing something other than a seal? Is a curious selkie in fact following me instead?

When I got back to my starting point, where the freshwater creek meets the sea, I sat down on a rock to see what would transpire. My companion didn't stay, though, for after seeing me settled I suppose she lost interest, or had more important things to do than entertain a mere mortal.

She bobbed up one last time, then vanished among a patch of floating seaweed. Being reluctant to let go of the experience and maybe a closer contact, I was sorry to see her leave, but leave she did. And to this day I remain in awe over that day's experience and hopeful of someday meeting again.

Victoria

Omen

In Celtic myth and legend, seals have a magical connection with humans, for seals—or selkies, as they were called—could transform themselves into men and women, an ability called skin-turning. It was believed if you found the skin of a selkie that had transformed itself, and you hid its skin, it could not return to the sea. But if that skin was later found, the selkie would forsake all for the call of the open waters and its old life as a seal.

Seals are associated with transformation, balance, and creativity. Seal lives in balance between the shore and the sea, spending time in both, so she calls for us to balance our own lives.

The shoreline is also the boundary between the material world and the mystical Celtic Otherworld where we can meet with our spirit guides, totem animals, and the faery realm. In this liminal place we can transform ourselves from the ordinary to the spectacular through these contacts.

Seal calls from the depths of the sea, making her way into our own world of artistic creativity, stimulating our imagination and showing us how to bring balance flowing into our lives. Listen to her call and look beyond the mundane toward a world just waiting to be discovered, a world full of vision, dreams, and Otherworld contacts. Seal is waiting for you to open the door to the possibilities.

SKUNK

WHEN I WAS A CHILD, my mother told me she would like to have a pet skunk. I always remembered that comment, so when I found six orphaned skunk babies, I was expecting a big smile when I presented my mother with the litter. Of course, I forgot to consider my mother's age: she was now seventy-six. So when I reminded her, "But you always wanted a skunk!" she reminded me, "That was fifty years ago."

Both of us were animal lovers, so our first concern was for the newborns' survival. We also wanted to get the smell off them, so we bathed them in tomato juice and warm water, then got them warm and dry. Next was making an appointment with my vet for de-scenting, and that didn't go well. The vet informed me that keeping skunks was illegal. Bring them in, he said, and he would put them to sleep. My mother and I talked it over and decided that was not an option. We had plenty of property. We would at least try to give them a chance at life.

A friend of my mother's, when told of the new residents, came over to help. She told us that years ago she found some baby skunks in her mailbox, placed there by some neighbor boys as a joke. One thing she discovered at that time was that skunks don't spray unless threatened or scared. This was a relief to us: all we had to do was keep them calm!

As for feeding . . . keeping six newborn skunks fed was a round-the-clock job. Friends helped us out, and fortunately, by the time the novelty wore off the skunks were old enough to sleep through the night without having to eat.

The next step was to introduce them to the great outdoors, where we hoped to return them someday. At the time I had three Siamese cats, and they all loved the little skunks. Being a bit of a nonconformist, I couldn't resist walking out to the mailbox every morning with the cats in front and the skunks bringing up the rear. I'd start out with a good laugh because the neighbors would do a double take, but not one of them ventured to open the windows to say hello.

At about six weeks the babies started to develop their own personalities. We also noticed that each one's stripe, at least on the forehead, was slightly different, which made naming them easier.

My favorite was R.S., short for Resident Skunk. From day one my husband, all six-foot-four of him, wouldn't have anything to do with the litter, and R.S. took great delight in trapping him. When my husband had to pass near the skunk, R.S. stamped his forefeet and turned his rear around as if to say, "I'm going to get you!" This was usually followed by the call, "Come get this damn skunk!"

We eventually lost a few, but R.S. remained with us for two years. I had not found my spiritual path yet, but years later I learned that Skunk teaches self-esteem and respect for ourselves as well as others. My self-esteem had certainly been lacking at the time, and whenever that little guy was with me I demanded respect without even knowing it.

The only real enemy a skunk has, other than humans, is the great horned owl. For years an owl had always visited my property around the end of October, but then he disappeared. It had been three years since I'd heard his call. That fall I was visited by a rogue skunk who took great delight in spraying under my house around three in the morning. Even with my past close association with skunks, I was losing patience, so I asked for Owl to return and teach this guy some manners.

A day later I heard the familiar *whoo-whoo* up in the top of his favorite pine tree. The skunk problem ended.

The owl stayed on about two weeks longer, then went his way.

I smiled and remembered my mother saying, "Careful what you wish for; you just may get it."

Sannee

Omen

Skunks seldom hurry. Their behavior reflects their life-style—slow and steady progress always takes them to their ultimate destination one way or another. They have no need to rush or throw their weight around to achieve their goals. By being who they are, they get what they seek because their self-esteem or sense of self is never in question.

Skunk can teach us how to get and give respect, whichever the situation calls for, but always through peaceful means and in the right way and time. They can also teach about boundaries and how to honor our own and others'—for crossing boundaries can stem from a need for power or a desire to control. Skunks know their own boundaries and demand respect for them. They normally go out of their way to avoid confrontation, but if necessary they don't hesitate to protect these boundaries if they have been crossed. Skunks are good examples of level-headedness and clear thinking.

If Skunk has crossed your path, ask yourself whether your self-esteem is lacking in some way. Do you rush around trying to do it all to impress others? Skunk could be telling you to slow down and cultivate your own self-esteem and self-respect.

Check your boundaries. Are they intact in a healthy way, or do they need shoring up because of neglect? Skunk can help you see where to use the natural forces of healing in your life to reestablish neglected boundaries. Stand tall and be who you were born to be.

SNAKE

MY SHORT-LIVED RELATIONSHIP HAD JUST ended. Not badly, but it seemed to me like another failure. I felt emotionally spent and desired solitude to walk and think out in nature, among my tree friends and the Goddess of this humble yet mystical grove. I needed nurturing, so I headed to the place I knew I could count on for that.

The creek that flows through the center of the park was plump and full, having caught the winter rains from the foothills. My emotions felt full also. I longed for clarity in handling them, so I walked down to the water's edge and knelt down to talk with the undines. They're the elementals associated with water and our emotional plane as humans. They help us absorb and assimilate life experiences, so I asked for help in understanding the emotional aspects of what had happened and how to deal with it. I left an offering in gratitude—lavender sprinkled into the flowing, circling creek. As I floated my hand in the water I could appreciate how water purifies and clears blockages that build up through our journey in life.

Standing up, I stepped along the bank before ascending the path, and there I saw, floating along the bottom of the creek, a small striped snake. The snake bobbed up and down slightly with the flow of the water. It looked to me like it was resting, or stunned. I couldn't tell.

Not being much of a snake expert, I wasn't sure what kind it was, if it would bite, or even if snakes could stay underwater long. I placed one end of my walking stick gently alongside the snake to see if it would move; it didn't, except to turn over on its back, belly up. This signified to me that, in whatever way, it was harmless, so I reached in and picked it up.

Then I realized it was a five-inch plastic toy snake that the water's current had distorted, making it appear very lifelike. Did I feel silly? Not in the slightest. I felt it was a sign of some sort, so I put it in my pocket and headed for home. I decided to research what it might signify.

As I studied the characteristics of snakes I found out quite a bit. The snake is associated with the continuing cycle of life, death, and rebirth. The ability to shed its skin mirrors this cycle, going from one step of life to another, transcending or leaving behind the old outmoded form for something new, something better.

The snake also symbolizes healing. Two snakes entwined around a central staff represent balance between two opposites: masculine and feminine, yin and yang, light and dark—for only through balance does true healing come, whether it's emotional, physical, or spiritual.

Snake also represents power and life force—the force in our bodies that is known as Kundalini in Eastern traditions, and the force the earth carries through the land as energy lines or ley lines.

Would you call my experience by the stream synchronistic, or an answer to a prayer? I called it clarity and understanding, for it enabled me to see I was moving closer to becoming self-actualized by each experience that helped me evolve, including the one I had just gone through. Do I doubt the gods sometimes use the simplest, most mundane means of getting our attention and helping us out? Absolutely not, for this time it came in the form of a toy snake, a creature of the water.

It's just a matter of being open to it and trying not to second-guess how the answers come.

Victoria

Omen

If you have met with Snake, prepare for death and rebirth in a symbolic form. You are being told that all things change, and you will soon shed some aspect of yourself that no longer serves you. You will exchange something no longer needed for something of more worth to you in the future—something that will help you become more truly yourself.

Standing firm and in balance, you can weather whatever you are called to change. Create healing energy through visualization, meditation, and grounding, and you will slip through this transformation with ease.

SQUIRREL

"LOOK UP," SAID MY COMPANION. "Look up and you'll learn something new today."

I stopped in the middle of the path and looked up. "Oh, it's only a gray tree squirrel, I see them all the time. Plus, she's eating—that's nothing new," I answered, and started to walk on.

"Will you quit being so stubborn and just watch for a minute?" Balthazar is generally right when he admonishes me to do something, so I shrugged off my impatience and looked again.

Sitting on a branch about fifteen feet up, the squirrel was nibbling on what seemed to be an acorn. She looked down at me, but she was obviously concentrating on the food between her forefeet. She chewed around the top, flipped it over, chewed at the bottom, flipped it again and started

103

nibbling at it like an ear of corn. Up one side, turn it, back up the other side: round and round it went. I enjoyed watching her meticulous nibbles, then I realized it wasn't an acorn.

"Hey, see that?" I said to Balthazar. "She's eating a mushroom. I've never seen the squirrels here eat anything but acorns. Didn't know they ate mushrooms. Cool!"

"Told you you'd learn something new today. Watch and you'll see something else."

The squirrel must have gotten tired of my staring at her, because now she put the mushroom firmly in her mouth and scurried along the branch. As she primed herself to leap into another tree, a woodpecker flew by and dove at her. She looked up at it, then jumped, mushroom still in place. She landed on the branch, then was off again.

The woodpecker wasn't letting her get away that easily, though, because every time she took a new leap she got dive-bombed by the determined woodpecker. I had to laugh, for I wasn't sure who was more determined now, the woodpecker chasing the squirrel, or the squirrel trying to get away from the woodpecker.

After six or seven leaps the squirrel dropped the mushroom and ran down the trunk of the tree she was in, then I lost track of her. The woodpecker seemed content, though, for he came to rest on one of the branches and started pecking at the tree, looking for bugs.

It had been an enlightening and entertaining spectacle, and I did learn something. Not only did I learn that squirrels eat mushrooms and woodpeckers like the thrill of the chase, but I was reminded that Balthazar was right again. He likes being right, and he likes to rub it in.

"Little Sister, when will you learn I have a lot to teach you if you'll just listen? Don't try to act surprised; you know I'm always right." And he snickered all the rest of the way down the path toward home.

Victoria

Omen

Squirrels are hard-working, playful creatures. They'll run and jump, chase and chatter with each other, but sometimes when a human has crossed their path and disturbed them, they'll let them know just how annoyed they are. They'll stamp a forefoot, flick their tail, and send out a tirade of squirrel chastisement—so don't bother a busy squirrel or you'll suffer the consequences.

Squirrels are known for their resourcefulness and preparedness for the future, for they always have their rainy-day supply well in order, stocking up food for the lean winter months. They are good examples of determination and planning ahead. And they don't dilly-dally around when they have a job to do; they get it done.

As an omen, Squirrel teaches not only about preparing for change of any sort but also how to deal with change when it comes around. Remember, squirrels don't sit and watch life happening around them; they are fully in the moment of living. Squirrels might not always deal with change calmly, but they don't let that change stop them from their goals or moving forward.

If Squirrel has scurried into your life, check to see if you are prepared for changes to come. This doesn't mean obsessively buying what you don't really need or being afraid of a "lack of." It means asking, do you have what you need to be comfortable, not only in material supplies but emotionally as well? Are you in balance and capable of being your own emotional and spiritual support?

Look to squirrel's example of planning and determination to make your life a more stable and healthy one.

STARFISH

I LEFT EVERYONE SLEEPING IN camp and headed for the beach. This morning I wanted to get a head start on all the other beachcombers and check out the tide pools by myself. The tide was out, and I knew the large inky-black rock would be accessible.

Walking along the water's edge, I was looking for shells and sea glass, turning over seaweed, dodging waves, and enjoying the taste of salty mist on my lips. A couple of sand crabs scurried out of some overturned seaweed and crawled around what was left of a jellyfish that had washed up on shore. I nudged it with my toe and watched its translucent body vibrate and shimmer. *It's gone the way of all living things eventually,* I thought. *Happy travelings,* I wished its spirit, and I continued on.

When I reached the rock, I carefully climbed on, making sure not to slip on the seaweed—it hangs on much better than I can—and crept up and over the top to the shallow tide pool that lay on the other side. Squatting down, I scanned the bottom of the pool, which was still clouded by the occasional wave that threw saltwater in and churned up the sand. Green sea anemones attached firmly in place . . . small rocks washed smooth and round . . . a crab trapped by the waning tide . . . and a big five-armed starfish, a big purple five-armed starfish—one of the prettier ones I'd seen. The perfectly formed arms were flecked with white nubs like splattered paint flung from an errant paintbrush. I bent down for a closer look.

In mythology, starfish are connected to the Star People and the Milky Way. The Milky Way was seen as streaming out from the breasts of the Goddess, turning part of the sky into a pearly white river. The sea is the origin of all life as we know it, so the sea is the great fertile womb of the Mother Goddess and the sky is the sustenance she offers, necessary to life and growth. In these realms she set her five-armed purple star for me to see and be reminded of her on the morning of my beachcombing.

"Hello, Starfish. Blessings of the morning." Turning to face the water, I sent out my gentlest loving energy toward the unrestrained intersection of sea and sky.

"My Lady of the Sea, Queen of the Starry Skies, bless your daughters and sons who walk upon this earth, your body. Help us strive to live in harmony and love with reverence and devotion to you, for some have become alienated from what we used to hold as sacred and divine. Thank you, Fair One, for allowing me to partake in your beauty and always helping me remember how blessed I truly am." And with that I sat down to meditate on the wonders of her creations.

The starfish held no deep meaning for me that morning except to remind me of our connection to the natural world and how she sustains all of us who reside on this finite body of hers. She provides for us continually and sometimes we forget that, for how easy it seems to happen, we take so much of living for granted. By being aware of the body of the goddess and connecting with her gentle rhythms of life and showing respect, we can find peace and harmony in a world filled with discord. I am reminded of that every time I see her wonders, and this morning was no exception. The starfish are just one of her perfect creations, and we are another. All that manifests upon this earthly plane comes from her essence, so we all have perfect potential. Yes, we are truly blessed if we would only realize it.

Victoria

Omen

Starfish, or sea stars as they are called by marine biologists, come in many colors and sizes, with the largest variety residing in the northern Pacific Ocean.

Most starfish have five arms, but some have up to twelve. Several species have the ability to regenerate lost arms; they can regrow a new one over a period of time.

Starfish do not have blood, but instead run seawater through their hard, spiny skeleton body. By living continually in the sea and using this salty brine as their lifeblood, starfish are physically aware of and connected to the tidal movements and the cycles of the moon. Hence they are associated with the moon and with sea magic.

With their star shapes and their attunement to the flux of the tides, starfish are also associated with the Milky Way and the gods and goddesses of sea and sky. Everything in our solar system is formed out of the dust of exploded stars, so the starfish reflects creation and union of the divine principles of male and female.

If you have seen Starfish, now could be your opportunity to get in tune with your own inner rhythms and flows, and to focus on your strengths.

Growth could also be on the horizon. You may need to acknowledge something that had been lost inside you, then bring it into the light and replace it with something better or more in tune with who you are now. Once you rediscover these lost elements you will be able to change something, some pattern or habit, in a way that also changes you, the people in your life, and the world around you. You are being called to regenerate what was lost.

TURKEY

"WANT TO GO FOR A ride down to the river? I'd like to see if any more of the bank has washed out."

Riding down to the river was my dad's and my favorite thing to do together. He liked to keep an eye on the river to see if it was getting any closer to changing course—as it had in 1937, when he was a boy. The shifting watercourse took out two hundred or more acres of leveled farmland, leaving the original waterway backed up with stagnant river. The only hand-operated water pump was submerged in the torrent of floodwater, making fresh water hard to come by for a while.

My dad's interest in the river also simply reflects his love for this area and his reminiscing about the freedom he enjoyed as a boy. I'll use any excuse to go along for the ride. I love to watch the changing landscape as we go from the city, with its sterile concrete buildings surrounded by life-less gray sidewalks, through neighborhoods of perfectly manicured lawns and chemically treated pools, into areas where houses lie farther apart and the countryside starts to stretch into long expanses of remote wildness.

As we drive along the river, it's like being in the midst of a familiar rural setting, but on my father's terms. Familiar because of the many stories I've heard about his roamings there, and also familiar because once you've reestablished your connection with the natural world you're welcomed anywhere that world extends to. It's like stepping into the open waiting arms of warm and loving friends.

Outside of town, the road gives us two options.

"You want to go left or right?"

Left leads back home. Right leads farther into the open rice fields and farmlands.

"Right, please. I want more countryside." So right we go. Outside the car window pass majestic gray-barked oaks, cottonwoods leafed out and fluttering green and silver in the breeze, elder branches bursting with tiny clusters of bluish fruit, wild grapevines tangled around sycamore trees with their white trunks peeling in brown flakes, and flame-orange poppies, our state flower. On it goes, laid out along the river, seemingly endless miles of beauty as we drive on, enjoying the sights and sounds of our home.

A bend in the road, and now we see a white house, obviously there a long time but still lovingly cared for, with a well-established walnut orchard squeezed into the riparian landscape. Then I spot the wild turkeys nestled four rows deep in the orchard, contentedly milling around in the shade and protection of the trees.

"Dad, look, are those wild turkeys? Yes, they are! Wait, wait, turn around." By this time we've traveled a quarter-mile down the road, but my pleading does the trick, and around we go.

Suddenly, bolting across the roadway run five, no eight, wait, *ten* turkeys, surging forward as if pushed from behind by a giant gust of wind. I gaze out over the car hood, enchanted by this bunch of wild, running, native members of our continent. Swiftly they dip out of sight into the field of rich, luxurious alfalfa. A pause, and then my last sighting: all in a row, at breakneck speed, the turkeys race for the cover of underbrush closer to the river.

As my father says something about heading back home, the bark of a scrub jay brings me out of my trance. Only for a moment had I been so entranced, but it was at that moment I felt perfect contentment, perfect stillness of mind, as if the world had passed me by except for my encounter with the turkeys. I longed to get out of the car and run after them, running down the current of the wind toward a freedom I knew lay out there in nature somewhere.

Instead I turned and smiled at my dad, breathing deep into my human body the air of this physical world. Back to the basics of living.

I am ever-grateful to my father for raising me with a love and respect for nature. And I'm grateful to all the teachers and guides along the paths of my life who helped reawaken my dormant knowing. I'm grateful for the guidance they let spill out to me, offering visions beyond the forces that hold this everyday world in place. I have learned so much, and the learning continues day after day with each encounter I have in my life. I pray I will be able to return that to others, to fill them with the sweet taste of life among the energies of the natural world and open their eyes to the beauty and connection that dwells there, waiting with those open arms.

Victoria

Omen

Turkey: harvest, abundance, autumn, and family. Apples, Thanksgiving, gourds, and pumpkins. These are just a few of the images the word *turkey* conjures up. The celebration of Thanksgiving is one generally held around hearth and home, and turkey plays a big part in this, for turkey gives of himself so others might continue.

Native to this continent, at one time wild turkeys were abundant. Hunting and human encroachment on their habitat put them in danger, but today the wild turkey population is again on the rise.

Turkeys are smart and elusive. Symbolizing sacrifice and the spirit of freedom, they remind us of the fundamentals of life on this planet Earth. When you honor Turkey, you honor the Earth Mother, for she provides, and Turkey is here to help us remember that.

If you have seen Turkey, be aware of the world that surrounds you. Turkey is telling you that you have much to be thankful for, even if you can't see it at the moment. Life is a wonderful gift, and the world is full of abundance. And not only do we receive, we can also give back. What are you giving back? How are you helping to replenish what's been given to you? What sorts of sacrifice have you honored? Turkey is asking you to be aware of the needs others have. Maybe you could donate your time to a charitable organization, or help take care of animals at the local humane society. Even picking up trash along the roadside shows a sacrifice of your time. Generosity sent out will be generosity returned.

Turkey says that genuine gratitude and willingness to give opens the door for the good to enter.

VULTURE

I WAS NOTHING MORE THAN an adult version of a toddler when I started on my spiritual path. My curiosity was insatiable, the instability of my newfound footing apparent by the trips and falls I took along the way. But I decided early on not to let any of these blind but innocent mistakes stop me. I simply got up, comforted my bruised ego, and moved forward in search of the answers somewhere else. Always I tried to remain open to the prompting and teachings from Spirit, my guides intervening on my behalf now and then to keep me from getting too wounded in the process.

So it was with profound wonder that I started paying closer attention to the birds and animals I met along the path of my journey. At first I only saw them as feathered or furry, flying here or scurrying there, but then something new took over, something I wasn't wholly familiar with. It was my first real encounter with a metaphysical aspect of something I considered mundane.

That morning, a cool breeze floated in and out of the tree branches, swaying them gently and lulling those roosted there into a soft half-slumber. Sitting on a rough wooden bench in the park, I looked down the long avenues of Italian cypress trees, all lined up in neat, tidy rows. It was a day of contemplation on my part. I was considering my place in the world, my lives in various times and places, and the ancestors that brought me to this point in my existence. I was hungry for answers and insights.

I glanced up to see the blue sky peering back at me in scattered places among the cypress branches. That's when I sighted something large and brown sitting in a treetop, on the uppermost branch. I shifted my seating to get a clearer picture. Whatever it was, it looked big. *Goodie, goodie!* my toddler mind laughed. *Something new, something big, something . . . scary?* Climbing onto the four-foot-tall railing that stood behind the bench, I craned my neck to one side. There it was, wings outstretched, back to the early morning sun: a turkey vulture.

Ooh, turkey vulture, was my first thought. *They eat dead things.* But as I sat watching, my feelings started to shift. Yes, this bird certainly was big, and not the prettiest thing around, but how dignified he was, and how still he sat, with his brown bi-colored feathers catching the light of the sun and reflecting it back as if to give it honor.

I lay back on the four-inch railing to watch for a while, floating in space, precariously balanced but anchored by the rail digging between my shoulder blades. As I looked up I could see the vulture had company, two others having the same experience with the sun. The breeze still blew; the trees still rocked. I could feel myself rocking, also, back and forth into a kind of consciousness that moves past time and space . . .

I was standing in a field of tall green grass and blue flowers whose swaying mirrored the rocking sensation I felt. As far as I could see there was only this vastness of blue and green, mingled on the horizon with the blue of the sky. Looking past this hazy line I had to squint ever so slightly, for the sun was directly overhead and sent down waves of light and heat that rippled on that selfsame breeze. This place seemed familiar to me . . . but then again it didn't.

I wasn't aware of moving, but now I was standing looking down at the face of a young girl not more than ten years old. She lay on her back surrounded by this field of flowers and grass, eyes closed, a half-smile on her face. As I watched she gradually rose off the ground, still reclining, stopped even with the tops of the grasses, hovered for a minute or two, then slowly descended back to the earth. She came to rest exactly where she had started.

I was taken aback, for I had never witnessed anyone levitate before. It was then that I realized this place definitely was not familiar, and what was I doing here . . . ?

Apparently I came back to my everyday consciousness with a start, for I almost fell off the railing, catching myself before taking the tumble. My heart pounded. Was I frightened or elated by what I had seen? Still in the toddler stage of my spiritual growth, I didn't know quite what to make of it all.

Sliding down from the railing, I glanced back up at the turkey vultures. One was still in the same position, one had moved slightly, and one had gone—where, I had no idea. I did remember to give my thanks to the vultures for letting me share in their sunning experience, and with that I went home to contemplate all that had happened on my new spiritual path.

A couple of months later, I had an appointment with a woman gifted with psychic abilities and seeing past lives. I didn't share with her my experience with the vultures or what I had seen in the field of flowers. But when she led me through a past-life regression, she herself saw the young girl lying in the field. She saw her rise up, too, but she also saw the girl's guardians telling her not to levitate in this time and place because other people were not ready to witness such gifts. So the girl never did it again, though she knew she could.

It turned out that this girl was an ancestor of mine. I had experienced an altered state of consciousness that day in the park. That state was prompted by my desire to learn and understand and my openness to Spirit, which moved hand in hand with the power of Vulture. I learned that the gift of levitation was still evident in my bloodline, but the knowing had been lost.

What an interesting development, then, along my new path. This news made my toddler feet wobbly with excitement. But at first, the power of the experience was overshadowed by my fear—fear of my first flight into the world of a different reality. I promptly put it out of my mind until a time when I felt stronger and more capable of handling it.

And now? No, I still haven't tried to perfect this gift yet. I think, even after all these years, that just the knowing will suffice. And then, maybe I'll leave it for my grandchildren to sort out.

Victoria

Omen

Commonly known as buzzards, vultures are considered dirty and offensive by some because they are carrion feeders and scavengers associated with death. But they're quite amazing birds. Vultures have their own methods for keeping themselves clean and healthy. Their digestive tracts contain chemicals that kill the bacteria present in the foods they eat. They bathe frequently and use the morning sun to cleanse themselves of any remaining bacteria. They also serve to prevent disease and infection from spreading to other animals, helping to keep the environment clean.

In flight, vultures can ride thermals and updrafts for hours without ever flapping their wings. Watching them, we can visualize what true freedom is, for Vulture teaches us how to soar and glide under our own energy.

Vulture is believed to hold the mysteries and secrets of levitation because of his ability to soar with no seeming movement. His apparent weightlessness, his release of the physical world, teaches us about letting go of the physical after death, the flight of the spirit to its true home amidst the Divine, the shift from one consciousness, the physical, to the other: the spiritual.

If you have spotted Vulture, now is the time to release your assumptions about what can and can't happen on this earthly plane. All things are possible in the world of Spirit; only our inability to let go of old obsolete conditioning holds us back.

If you ache to touch the mystical, Vulture has come to teach how to uncover truths and clarify the misconceptions that keep us trapped in outmoded belief systems.

Let the subliminal work through you. Stay sensitive to that which is below your normal everyday awareness. Vulture will help you uncover the part of your consciousness that allows you to let go of the mundane. Vulture will help you see the secrets of nature that are held out to you if you are willing to grasp them. Don't be content with the usual when the magical is so very close.

WHITE HART

HUNGER WILL CAUSE PEOPLE TO do things they wouldn't normally do. For years I've hesitated to retell this story. But now that the end is closer, I'm hoping to come to terms with the guilt I feel about it. I hope to free myself to go my way in peace.

There was a great hunger going on back then, and not just for me and mine. I was twelve, the oldest boy left at home in a family of eight. Mom stayed home trying her best to raise us with no money and not much means of getting any. Dad cut wood when he could find work at it, but was rarely home. We were always hungry, most of the time finding nothing in our lunch pails but day-old biscuits, hard from start to finish.

We lived way out past any towns, paved roads, or usual conveniences, and our only company were the animals, birds, and such that dwelled in the forests and groves. The one comfort I found in life was hunting game along the river and among the trees that had stood there long before people came that way to make their homes.

On this day, I grabbed my .22 and set out, headed for wherever my feet would take me. Soon I was walking through a thick grove of oak trees, nestled among outlying willows and cottonwoods. I stood still when I heard a noise from deep in the center of the grove. Then I saw it. The outline of a deer: food for the table. We would eat tonight.

I dropped to my hands and knees, creeping forward every time the deer lowered its head to eat. I was about twenty feet from where it stood when the deer caught wind of me. By this time I could see that this was no ordinary deer but a perfect white stag, tall and majestic, the sun glistening off its coat. I was so mesmerized that I had no choice but to chase after it when it started to run. Hunger, shock, and awe compelled me on. I lifted my rifle and fired, but the stag kept running and running through the forest, and I kept chasing after it. Then it started to slow down, and in a clearing among the oaks it fell sideways, red blood staining its white coat and the ground where it lay.

The word *remorse* cannot begin to describe how I felt at that moment. Feelings unknown to me as a boy of twelve rolled through my heart and stomach. I felt sick and heavy.

What had I done, and what should I do now? My family needed to eat, so I had hunted the deer, but I had not understood that my feelings over what had transpired would manifest in this way.

I ran to find my father, hoping he would be at the campsite he stayed at once in a while. He was there, and I told him the story, hoping to gain some form of comfort in the telling. Then we set out to butcher the deer and bring home the meat for our family. Those meals alleviated our hunger for a few nights, but the pain in my heart has never subsided.

All these years have passed and I still look back with regret over taking the life of that beautiful creature. I've since asked forgiveness from the deer and also blessed it for feeding us. That experience could probably never happen twice for a twelve-year-old boy. But if it had, I cannot honestly say I would hunt the deer again, no matter how hungry I was.

You tell me the deer consciously gave its life so we could eat? I'd like to believe that, because it is a small comfort. I hope you're right.

Anonymous

Omen

The stag is associated with Cernunnos, the Celtic god of the animals and god of the hunt. Cernunnos is depicted with antlers on some ancient archeological finds throughout Europe.

Since deer shed their antlers in December and regrowth begins in spring and summer, the antlered god represents growth, fertility, new life, and inner illumination. He is the fully actualized energy of the season in all its strength and vitality.

In some indigenous societies it's believed that if you hunt a white animal and partake of its flesh, you take on its spirit; the animal gives away to you. You and the animal are one, and it becomes your totem animal, your protector and guide, who carries with it the magic and knowledge of the faery realm and guards its gateway.

> The White Hart or white stag was an Otherworldly animal. In many myths, a mysterious white hart appears to the hero, challenging him to hunt it through the forest. It may lead the hero into the Otherworld. The stag turns out to be his own soul, and the hunt a necessary lesson. What does the spiritual hunter hunt? He hunts his own true Self. The fate of the antlered King, like the white stag symbolised the soul growth that required radical changes on all levels of consciousness.*

---

* Anna Franklin, *Familiars: Animal Powers of Britain* (Milverton, England: Capall Bann Publishing, 1997), page 140. Used with permission.

If the White Hart has come to you, expect a visit from the Otherworld. Your life is about to change dramatically.

WHITE-TAILED KITE

FIBROUS RED TRUNKS, LONG NEEDLELIKE leaves, and deep furrowed brows carved from long-held wisdom: all gaze toward me as I stand within the perfect circular grove of redwood trees.

Sophia acts as the sentinel for this mighty group of grove guardians here in the woods. She has the love and willingness to allow me to merge my energy with hers, forming one perfect energetic vibration.

I stand with eyes closed, feeling the energy and peace that floats like soft dandelion seeds on the wind. Deep inside me, deep where my hopes and dreams reside, I am poised on the verge of taking the step into actualizing something I have long hoped for but almost abandoned time after time. I have come here to strengthen my resolve, to seek the power to resist dumping the project yet again. I have come for merging, and insight, and added strength to hold firmly to my plans. I have come seeking hope.

I inhale the fresh fragrance of redwood and feel the energy as it rises, heavier than before. It swirls the layers of tiny flecks of vibration around and around the circle, penetrating into my body, going deeper into the area of my hopes and dreams—and fears. The fears that always surface whenever I try to slip out of my comfortable, well-worn ruts. Now they surface again: twisted black faces snarl around me; their icy teeth grabbing and clutching at my knees and ankles, binding them with steely chains that grip hard and hold me back.

"Not now! Daddy, Mommy, I'm spinning again," I call out in my childhood terror. "The monsters of the closet are ready to grab me. I can't breathe. Help!"

But just as I'm about to surrender to my dusty, fear-filled inner closet, I sense a movement to my left and open my eyes in time to catch a white flash rising breathlessly from the cover of Sophia's green needle-strewn branches. All around me, the energy drops slowly down into the earth. I feel tired, weary of carrying the weight of these chains around my ankles. But instead of resting, I move on, following after the white streak that flew up and away from the redwood grove.

Minutes go by, but all I see are the sunlit forest and the blue of the sky. I stop by a walnut tree. "Where have you gone?" I ask aloud. I am determined to discover where this ghostly presence has flown while I was suspended between past and present.

Now, from somewhere high above, the white streak descends, at full speed, straight at me. It's a bird, and elation overtakes me. I've not seen any white birds in this area except for an occasional seagull. Is this a gull? Disappointment sets in. Nothing against seagulls, I was just hoping for something different, something more. Prompted by some need to continue to observe it, I stand stone-still while the bird slides closer into view. It sweeps up and over my head, rising higher, then stops, wings flapping the rhythm of instinct, breast and head pointed downward, talons extended, ready to strike. Hovering, hovering in midair. Not the action of a seagull; this is a bird of prey.

"What are you hunting, white one? Surely not me." At the mention, it flies off effortlessly towards the top of Sophia and her clan, where it comes to rest contentedly beside another white bird.

Now I hear words addressed to me. "The time has come for you to own your power and take your place with grace, dignity, and humbleness."

I was hunted; we all are. Hunted by our own true selves: the Shaman, the Priestess, the White Knight, the Druid, those of love and wisdom who are willing to go where the need is to serve the earth and humanity.

Our inner being, in its truth and purity, is held back by layer upon layer of mind and body and subconscious chatter. We lie naked and vulnerable in the mud of fear, longing to be released, to fly above what we are in physical form, past what holds us back and keeps us chained.

And so it is, and so it was. I went home that day with a new determination not to give in to my long-held fears, but to use them to propel me forward. The white birds—they were white-tailed kites—were sent to show me the way out of my dark tangled inner pains of past, present, and future fears.

Victoria

Omen

The white-tailed kite symbolizes the powers of the mind, such as higher awareness and new vision. Kite will teach us understanding, truth, and spiritual lessons that can be used to help us move forward on our life path.

If Kite has come, it's urging you to make your bid for freedom from fear by allowing new understandings to flow into your life.

Sometimes what holds us back and blocks our progress is our fear of the unknown, the untried: we fear for the safety of the child inside of us. Know that, amidst all the changes we undergo, all the new understanding we acquire, all the higher wisdom we attain, we are always protected and guided along the way. We are watched over and helped through the tough times as we listen with our inner hearing to the voice of the Divine, the voice that encourages us to move forward in our quest for balance and wholeness.

WOODPECKER

A FLASH OF RED, WHITE, and black feathers blurred against the green of the leaf-clustered branches. Oakmarr, the stately Valley Oak, smiled in his own warm way and sent off his happiest energy as the tri-colored woodpecker careened from branch to branch in a flurry of activity. I looked up into Oakmarr's canopy. Some of his twisting branches rose up toward the amberina sky, others veered down toward the cool moisture hugging the earth where he stood rooted.

I lay back on the bench at the base of the tree, intent on staying informed of the activity going on above my head. Settling in, I watched as the woodpecker came to rest on a branch devoid of leaves but littered with dime-sized holes running along its woody arm.

Waka-waka-waka, the woodpecker noisily announced. "Stay away, I'm hunting for food, stay away."

I laughed. "No one to bother you from down here. Up there's another story, though."

Thump-thump-thump-thump-thump, came the reply, then a moment of silence. *Waka-waka-waka.* "I'll share with you my grubby bugs. Meet me on the branch. I'll share."

"Thank you, my feathered friend, but your dinner does not sound as appealing as mine waiting at home." I swung my feet off the bench and stood up. "I mean no offense."

"None taken, but try it first. Yes, try it first."

It was difficult for me to somehow graciously decline partaking in the hospitality offered, when it was so freely offered. But I had come to understand that when journeying in another reality it's best not to eat or drink anything while there, grubby bugs included!

"Enjoy your dinner, woodpecker, and may all your meals be plentiful."

Stepping out from under Oakmarr and onto the path, I headed toward the tall straight pine trees, clusters of green pungent bay, through the zelkovas, then toward the cork oaks for home.

Thump-thump-thump-thump-thump, the rhythm went on behind me. *Waka-waka-waka.* "Stay away, I'm hunting for food, stay away."

I smiled to myself and took a moment to try to readjust to my everyday reality. "Funny woodpecker. He's sure to have the whole forest on his doorstep! He can't make that kind of noise for long without drawing attention, showing he's found a cache. But maybe that's his intent."

As I walked, the last vestiges of his world slowly slipped from me and dissipated into tree and rock, melting like low luminous fog in a sudden rain.

When we weave our life with another reality, we might view it as surrendering our humanity and our desire for control, as becoming willing and open to what other forms have to teach, and as learning how to play again. Being aware and present in Woodpecker's world, I was able to step beyond the mundane view that life is only three-dimensional and that humans are at the top of the evolutionary heap. There are always things human sight doesn't see—other levels of awareness.

Woodpecker can help us open those unseeing eyes and take off our blinders to find that sometimes the mysteries are hidden in obvious places. Woodpecker is always willing to take you to where these mysteries can be discovered.

I am never surprised anymore by what comes. It's always a wonderful journey, and what more could anyone ask for than an offering of grubby bugs? I doubt he would have accepted my offer of taco salad either, but you never know.

Victoria

Omen

Woodpeckers are wise forest dwellers that have knowledge of plants, animals, and the world of nature's workings. They are attuned to the rhythms of life. From high in their treetop homes, they beat in harmony with the pulsing heartbeat of the earth below.

In ancient times, woodpeckers were consulted as oracles, known to predict the weather in some places around Europe, where they are called "rain birds." They are said to know where treasures are hidden and where to find magical herbs for use in healing.

If Woodpecker has come, he has a message, some wisdom he needs to impart if you're willing to accept it. He can help you access the inner secrets of nature's workings and illuminate the places kept hidden from those who cannot see with fayland sight or hear with fayland ears.

Listen to Woodpecker's drumming rhythms and hear his voice, then feel the rhythm of life all around you. It is telling you to fine-tune your own inner song, for music is everywhere: just sing yours into existence. Even the softest note can have an impact, and woodpecker can be a willing participant.

EPILOGUE

A RUSTLING OF DRY LEAVES rose up from the thickly covered path as I picked my way toward a grove of mountain ash and oaks. The colors lay warm and golden, interspersed with rich dark brown earth, basking under a high sun. Up ahead, the path eased right toward a small rise that stood out against the otherwise flat expanse of land. A breast-high tumble of broom edged along the side of the path, finally wending its way down an embankment toward a trickling spring that oozed out of a cavity in the ground. I called toward the tree grove—to hear nothing in return but my own echo running back at me. Even before I reached it, I knew I was alone, with or without ever hearing a returning voice from the canopy of branched oaks.

As I managed my way off the path and through the broom toward the grove, a rising fragrance filled the air, light and fresh, like sweet honeysuckle floating in morning dew. I was being greeted. Some would say a wisp of cologne had floated on a little breeze and swept across the landscape, but I knew better. The Fair Folk greet as they may, generally inclined towards subtleties. Yet sometimes, if you're caught off guard, the greeting can take the form of a smack across the face—the force of their power leaving you wondering if you'd made the right decision in seeking them out.

The Fair Folk come and go at will and in seconds, so my perceived aloneness was correct at that moment in time. But their recognition of time is not ours. When you move through dimensions and shift planes, existence (or our vision of it) is a matter of vibrational energies moving in flux with all that is—essence. It's not something easily learned, as those who walk between the worlds will attest. But learn it you can. All it takes is persistent hard work and effort, lots of personal discipline, a fair amount of pain, mixed with occasional bouts of elation and frustration—plus a desire to reawaken what has lain dormant inside you. It's not a path for the faint-hearted, however.

More slowly now, I inched my way down the slight incline and around the spring. The jays flew high, barking their annoyance at my intrusion, almost in tune with the chatter the gray squirrels sent up at the feathered outburst. I caught sight of movement on my left and instinctively turned in that direction. It had grown quiet, so quiet that all I could hear was my own breath.

Then, stepping out of the cover of the trees, I saw her. The sun suddenly disappeared behind a passing cloud, leaving the grove drained of color, but a lingering shred of light caught her face, lovely as the first bloom of a pale pink rose. As prepared as I thought I had been, I was caught off guard by her appearance. It happens every time, and I always think I am used to it, but the force of the awe that surrounds me when in her presence is one that is never easy to fully anticipate.

As the breeze wove through the branches, it caught in bits of her hair, lifting it toward the light that lay across her face. She tilted her head slightly and laughed, smiling at me. Her laugh was the sound of a thousand rays of color filtering through crystal prisms, floating on gentle air currents, descending like drops of silvery sparkles in the night sky; it had the velvety touch of the Oran Mór, the music of creation. I stood in wonder before her.

"My Lady, my longing for your presence sent me out. The day was so beautiful I came searching for you in Eamhain Abhlach, the land of apples."

She stood silent for just a moment, then said, "And so I am here. What is it you seek of me?" The sound of her voice rang out from her heart, clear and pure, and at that very moment the sun burst through the cloud, filling the grove with brilliant yellow and orange light.

With this manifestation of power come from the heavens, I was caught completely tongue-tied. I stumbled upon the words in answer to her question, trying to get them to convey a sense of logic, but all I could manage was a sort of inaudible squeak. I was not afraid, but when I finally found my tongue again, I spoke as if I were.

"The mourning dove came to me," I replied, "and took me high on a hill where the air was softer and warmer than in the valley where I live. It was faintly scented, but I could not tell with what. It seemed a pungent smell of sharp tangy moss lain long underwater, warm mud, and ripe blackberry fruit. I could sense the dove had something to tell me, but I did not understand his language, for he was speaking in a tongue long dead. I felt I should have known it but didn't. It seemed so familiar, like part of my past that had moved sharply away from me at that very second. I dismissed it at the time, but lately it has caused me to wonder." I paused, looking to where she had seated herself on an oak stump.

Suddenly I was enveloped by a longing I could not describe. Deep inside me it had welled up, surrounding my heart with a single desire, a desire for union. It went past human contact, past time, or space, or beingness. There are no words, no tongues, no structures to express it: it was simply a desire to be wrapped safely in a cocoon with the great spark of creation, back to merge with the whole.

I watched over her shoulder as a squirrel skittered down a tree trunk, landing in a pile of soft reddish-gold leaves.

She waited for me to speak again. I could see the knowing in her eyes, her gentle understanding of the mysteries and secrets long held through time. Again I fell tongue-tied, but this time from uncertainty. How could I continue with this heaviness resting upon my breast?

She must have sensed my despair, for she rose and walked to me, speaking gently as she moved closer. "You see what is dealt with when in the human condition?" she said. "Most feel lost, not knowing the true purpose of life or where to seek for the answers, wandering in a kind of mind-numbing daze. All live by it, but not all come to question it. Those who do start to see glimpses of what lies on the other side of mundane physical existence, philosophies held for only the most enlightened seekers. You have come to that fork in your life's path, the path of the dove."

She paused to let me consider what she was saying, then continued. "The role the dove has chosen is to be a teacher for those ready to embark upon a quest for higher knowledge and personal direction. The dove's only concern is for the individual who has grown beyond the materialistic sides of life, one who has begun transcending ego and seeks to contact Divine Spirit. It is often a lonely path, but it can only be undertaken singly. It tests the seeker as to worthiness and purity of heart. Dove has come to you with a challenge. Do you feel ready to undertake it? For this journey will change you."

How could I answer that? Was I ready? Is this why I had come searching for her? I didn't honestly know. I could feel the fear rising inside me, a fear that held a lack of self-confidence, a sense of unworthiness, and an uncertainty about my own preparedness. Could I carry the responsibility of it all? Did I have the strength, and did I really want to change?

"I cannot hold you to whichever choice you make," she said. "But consider all that is being presented, for this will be an important lesson. In the end it will affect more than just yourself."

I could see her patiently waiting for my answer, and I watched her without thought, just a kind of blankness poised on the edge of clarity.

The snap of a twig brought me around. I turned and saw someone coming in my direction. Think fast! But when I turned back around to answer, she was gone. Melting away like a flame dying among the embers.

Silent I stood, concealed by the shadows of the oaks. I could see an old man veer away now, back toward the path. He seemed out of place in his gray dress pants and blue shirt, but then I must have seemed the same, standing there silently trying to hide from prying eyes.

My excursion had brought me answers, plus a fair number of interesting questions. So in the days that followed, I found I reflected more and more on my place in life. I grew stronger and more certain of where my path would take me, and I eventually followed it to this book. I put pen to paper to write about the animal encounters I have been entrusted with, placing them into story form, hoping to convey the messages that were given.

Each of us has a particular path to follow, and this is where mine led. I had come to this point in my life through plenty of trial and error. Sometimes I walked with confidence and surety; sometimes I fell blindly, bloodying my knees—but it was all held tightly in place by my spiritual roots and connection with the earth. We can all reclaim and nurture this connection if we choose to, no matter where we've been, or where we are now, on our life path.

I hope these stories help you, the reader, in that process. This book doesn't offer the last word on animal omens; it is simply another avenue for prompting ideas and insights into the relationships between humans, animals, and Otherworld entities. Take what is useful, and disregard the rest.

As you walk your own path through the world of nature, as each foot falls upon the sacred earth, take the time to also remember the animals, for they share our world. And remember Her, too. I hope you can hear her calling to you through mist and memory. And I hope you take the time to listen.

APPENDIX ONE

ANIMAL POWERS AND ATTRIBUTES

ANT

Community, order, discipline, patience, trust, industriousness, planning, determination, contentment, organization.

BEAVER

Family, home, industriousness, teamwork, achievement, goals, harmony, accomplishment.

BUTTERFLY

Otherworld guide, shape-shifter, the mind and mental clarity, beauty, soul flight, dreams, ancestral spirits, rebirth, spirit helper, change.

CAT

Sacred to the Goddess and associated with the moon. The ability to see and work in the spirit-world, guardian of Otherworld treasures, conduits for traveling between the worlds, independence, protection, fertility, prophecy, magic, psychic abilities, weather augury, heightened awareness.

CROW

Guardian of the gateway between beginnings and endings, past-life knowledge, keeper of sacred laws, magic, illusion, weather augury, shape-shifting, prophecy, death, protection, change, higher wisdom, dimensional shifts.

DEER

Gentleness, divination, shape-shifting, fertility, subtlety, the Otherworld/Faery Realm, spirituality, compassion.

DOG

Guards the roads and pathways, guards the mysteries, love, faithfulness, protection, companionship, guidance, loyalty, healing, service, devotion, compassion.

DRAGON

Air, Earth, Fire, Water, connection with the Otherworld, passion, unconscious mind, transmutation, depth of feeling, human potential, power, alchemy, energy, the psyche, grounding, treasures, reincarnation, higher levels of consciousness, mastery, inspiration, insight, guardianship, Kundalini.

DUCK
Betwixt and between times, emotions, astral plane, good fortune, feminine energies, healing, Otherworld travel, tranquility, peace.

EGRET
Balance, decisiveness, surety, evolution, exploration, innate wisdom, self-reflection, esoteric wisdom, patience, focus.

FOX
The ability to go within, knowledge of traveling between the worlds, learning to know oneself, cunning, natural world, wildness, clear vision, good fortune, invisibility, observation, adaptability, family, humor, charm, knowledge, decisiveness, joy.

HAWK
Solar gods, guardianship, illumination, messenger, visionary powers, protection, inspiration, prophecy, insight, observation, heightened awareness, ancestors, nobility, power of recollection, strength, knowledge.

HORSE

The ability to travel to different realms of consciousness, the land, journey, exploration, energy, inner realms, connections, wealth, good luck and fortune, life-cycle, fertility, transcending mortality, power, wisdom, dreamwalking, balance, freedom, divination, clairvoyance, sexuality, goals, bonds between friends and family.

HUMMINGBIRD

Joy, wonder, relationships, knowledge, flexibility, past lives, playfulness, fertility, love, beauty, happiness, creativity.

MOUNTAIN LION

Leadership, balance, power, grace, truth, responsibility, strength, decisiveness.

NEWT

The Otherworld/Faery Realm, adaptability, growth, emotion, renewal, balance, regeneration, intuition, transformation, spirituality.

OSPREY

Inner self, understanding, knowledge, insight, purification, self-reflection, ability to transcend.

OWL

Threshold guardian, higher wisdom, heightened senses, feminine energies, magic, prophecy, astral projection, illumination, change, intuition, clairvoyance, objectivity, secrecy, death, birth, discernment, protection, divination, spirituality, enlightenment, altered states of consciousness.

RABBIT

The ability to act and think fast, intuition, fertility, healing, new life, agility, the Faery Realm, sexuality, fear, doubt, luck, magic.

SEAL

The Otherworld/Faery Realm, balance, the unconscious, shape-shifting, magic, dreams, creativity, feminine energy, inspiration, transformation.

SKUNK

Respect, self-esteem, protection, boundaries, peace of mind, self-assurance, sensuality, confidence, adaptability.

SNAKE

Kundalini, life-death-rebirth cycle, initiation, higher wisdom, healing, transformation, alchemy, inner sight, knowledge, guardianship, change, movement, sexual energy/life-force energy, fertility, physical and metaphysical procreation.

SQUIRREL

Foresight, concentration, goals, preparedness, imagination, sociability, balance, achievement, change, determination.

STARFISH

Moon and sea magic, moon and sea gods and goddesses, balance, dreams, feminine energy, regeneration, cosmic consciousness, inner vision.

TURKEY

The earth, the Goddess. Sacrifice, family, honor, gratitude, sharing, harvest, freedom, service.

VULTURE

Purification, death, rebirth, levitation, grounding, strength, power, masculine energy, clear vision, patience, spirituality, clairfragrance, alchemy.

WHITE HART

Solar symbol, the Otherworld, journey, change, knowledge, wisdom, symbolic death and rebirth, strength, illumination, sacrifice, visions, the unconscious, growth, fertility, new life, protection.

WHITE-TAILED KITE

The mind, higher awareness, truth, insight, spiritual lessons, knowledge, strength, power.

WOODPECKER

Fertility, rebirth, weather augury, shape-shifting, hidden treasures, oracle bird, wisdom, the world of nature, herbalism, earth energies, rhythm, knowledge, insight.

APPENDIX TWO
ELEMENT ASSOCIATIONS

AIR

Crow, Deer, Hawk, Owl, Squirrel, Butterfly, Horse, Snake, Vulture, Hummingbird, White-Tailed Kite, Dragon.

EARTH

Deer, Dog, White Hart, Snake, Cat, Fox, Rabbit, Horse, Ant, Seal, Skunk, Turkey, Beaver, Dragon.

FIRE

Cat, Fox, Hawk, Snake, Egret, Woodpecker, White Hart, Rabbit, Horse, Newt, Squirrel, Mountain Lion, Vulture, Dragon.

WATER

Starfish, Egret, Horse, Duck, Snake, Woodpecker, Seal, Osprey, Beaver, Newt, Dragon.

Note: Some animals are associated with one or more elements.

Free Catalog

Get the latest information on
our body, mind, and spirit products!
To receive a **free** copy of Llewellyn's consumer
catalog, *New Worlds of Mind & Spirit,* simply call
1-877-NEW-WRLD or visit our website at
www.llewellyn.com and click on *New Worlds.*

LLEWELLYN ORDERING INFORMATION

Order Online:
Visit our website at www.llewellyn.com, select your books, and
order them on our secure server.

Order by Phone:
- Call toll-free within the U.S. at 1-877-NEW-WRLD
  (1-877-639-9753). Call toll-free within Canada at
  1-866-NEW-WRLD (1-866-639-9753)
- We accept VISA, MasterCard, and American Express

Order by Mail:
Send the full price of your order (MN residents add 6.5% sales tax)
in U.S. funds, plus postage & handling to:

Llewellyn Worldwide
2143 Wooddale Drive, Dept. 978-0-7387-1377-9
Woodbury, MN 55125-2989

Postage & Handling:

Standard (U.S., Mexico, & Canada). If your order is:
$24.99 and under, add $3.00
$25.00 and over, FREE STANDARD SHIPPING

AK, HI, PR: $15.00 for one book plus $1.00 for
each additional book.

International Orders (airmail only):
$16.00 for one book plus $3.00 for each additional book

Orders are processed within 2 business days.
Please allow for normal shipping time. Postage and handling rates subject to change.

Animal Speak

*The Spiritual & Magical Powers
of Creatures Great & Small*

TED ANDREWS

The animal world has much to teach us. Some animals are experts at survival and adaptation, some never get cancer, and some embody strength and courage, while others exude playfulness. Animals remind us of the potential we can unfold, but before we can learn from them, we must first be able to speak with them.

In this book, myth and fact are combined in a manner that will teach you how to speak and understand the language of the animals in your life. *Animal Speak* helps you meet and work with animals as totems and spirits—by learning the language of their behaviors within the physical world. It provides techniques for reading signs and omens in nature so you can open yourself to higher perceptions and even prophecy. It reveals the hidden, mythical, and realistic roles of 45 animals, 60 birds, 8 insects, and 6 reptiles.

Animals will become a part of you, revealing to you the majesty and divinity in all life. They will restore your childlike wonder of the world and strengthen your belief in magic, dreams, and possibilities.

978-0-87542-028-8
400 pp., 7 x 10, illus., photos $21.95

To order, call 1-877-NEW-WRLD

Prices subject to change without notice

Beyond 2012

A Shaman's Call to Personal Change and the Transformation of Global Consciousness

JAMES ENDREDY

War, catastrophic geological events, Armageddon . . . The prophecies surrounding 2012—the end of the Mayan calendar—aren't pretty. James Endredy pierces the doom and gloom with hope and a positive, hopeful message for humankind.

For wisdom and guidance concerning this significant date, Endredy consults Tataiwari (Grandfather Fire) and Nakawe (Grandmother Growth)—the "First Shamans." Recorded here is their fascinating dialogue. They reveal how the evolution of human consciousness, sustaining the earth, and our personal happiness are all interconnected.

Discover what you can do to spur the transformation of human consciousness. See how connecting with our true selves, daily acts of compassion and love, focusing personal energy, and even gardening can make a difference. Endredy also shares shamanistic techniques to revive the health of our planet . . . and ourselves.

978-0-7387-1158-4
240 pp., 7½ x 9⅛, four pages of full-color photos $16.95

Animal Magick

The Art of Recognizing &
Working with Familiars

D. J. CONWAY

The use of animal familiars began long before the Middle Ages in Europe. It can be traced to ancient Egypt and beyond. To most people, a familiar is a witch's companion, a small animal that helps the witch perform magick, but you don't have to be a witch to have a familiar. In fact, you don't even have to believe in familiars to have one. You may already have a physical familiar living in your home in the guise of a pet. Or you may have an astral-bodied familiar if you are intensely drawn to a particular creature that is impossible to have in the physical. There are definite advantages to befriending a familiar. They make excellent companions, even if they are astral creatures. If you work magick, the familiar can aid by augmenting your power. Familiars can warn you of danger, and they are good healers.

Most books on animal magick are written from the viewpoint of the Native American. This book takes you into the exciting field of animal familiars from the European Pagan viewpoint. It gives practical meditations, rituals, and power chants for enticing, befriending, understanding, and using the magick of familiars.

978-1-56718-168-5
288 pp., 6 x 9

$15.95

Four Seasons of Mojo
An Herbal Guide to Natural Living

STEPHANIE ROSE BIRD

The changing of the seasons can feel magical—greens changing to browns and golds, snow melting to show fresh buds. We all recognize these tell-tale signs, but few are aware of the powerful impact each season has on our spiritual lives. *Four Seasons of Mojo* infuses ancient techniques, rituals, and methods from around the world to use each season's inherent energies to supplement body, mind, and soul.

Designed to further spiritual practices by learning from neighboring cultures, this book provides readers with useful ideas unrestricted by geographic borders, ethnicity, religion, or magical path. Included are recipes and concepts from the Caribbean, African American soul food, Buddhist Meditation practices, sacred Hindu rites, Old European traditions, Australian Aboriginal dreaming lessons, and Native American wisdom.

978-0-7387-0628-3
240 pp., 7½ x 9⅛ $16.95

To order, call 1-877-NEW-WRLD
Prices subject to change without notice

The Outer Temple
of Witchcraft

Circles, Spells, and Rituals

CHRISTOPHER PENCZAK

As you enter the heart of witchcraft, you find at its core the power of sacred space. In Christopher Penczak's first book, *The Inner Temple of Witchcraft*, you found the sacred space within yourself. Now *The Outer Temple of Witchcraft* helps you manifest the sacred in the outer world through ritual and spellwork. The book's twelve lessons, with exercises, rituals, and homework, follow the traditional Wiccan one-year-and-a-day training period. It culminates in a self-test and self-initiation ritual to the second degree of witchcraft—the arena of the priestess and priest.

978-0-7387-0531-6
448 pp., 7½ x 9⅛, illus. $19.95

Earth, Air, Fire & Water

More Techniques of Natural Magic

SCOTT CUNNINGHAM

Selling over 200,000 copies, *Earth, Air, Fire & Water* features more than 75 spells, rituals, and ceremonies. Cunningham reveals the secrets of the four magical elements, in addition to the fifth one: spirit. He explores their basic nature and the types of rituals associated with each element. Herbs, stones, metals, musical instruments, colors, seasons, direction, and symbols corresponding with each element are also discussed. This bestselling guide to natural magic also introduces the basics of magic—concepts, techniques, and tools—to those who are new to the practice.

978-0-87542-131-5
240 pp., 5³⁄₁₆ x 8 $9.95

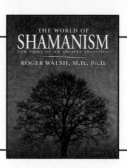

The World of Shamanism
New Views of an Ancient Tradition

ROGER WALSH, M.D., PH.D.

After decades of being demonized by clergy, pathologized by psychiatrists, and dismissed by academics, shamanism is thriving. So, what is fueling the West's new fascination with shamanism?

You'll find the answer and more in this objective exploration of shamanism and its place in contemporary life. Dr. Roger Walsh leaves no stone unturned as he examines shamanistic traditions throughout history, and how they intersect with modern psychology and metaphysical studies.

Are shamans enlightened or psychotic? Decide for yourself as Dr. Walsh unveils the life and mind of this revered figure. Delve into shamanic practices—healing, altered states of consciousness, journeying, channeling, vision quests—and discover if, how, and why they actually work. This cross-cultural, all-encompassing perspective will help you understand shamanism—its impact throughout history and its significance today.

978-0-7387-0575-0
336 pp., 7½ x 9⅛ $18.95

In the Shadow of the Shaman
Connecting with Self, Nature & Spirit

AMBER WOLFE

Presented in what the author calls a "cookbook shamanism" style, this book shares recipes, ingredients, and preparation methods for experiencing some very ancient wisdoms, drawing from Native American and Wiccan traditions and other philosophies of nature as they are used in the shamanic way. Wheels, the circle, totems, shields, directions, divinations, spells, care of sacred tools, and meditations are all discussed. Wolfe encourages us to feel confident and free to use her methods to cook up something new, completely on our own. This blending of ancient formulas and personal methods represents what Wolfe calls Aquarian Shamanism.

In the Shadow of the Shaman is designed to communicate in the most practical, direct ways possible, so that the wisdom and the energy may be shared for the benefits of all. Whatever your system or tradition, you will find this to be a valuable book, a resource, a friend, a gentle guide, and support on your journey. Dancing in the shadow of the shaman, you will find new dimensions of Spirit.

978-0-87542-888-8
384 pp., 6 x 9, illus. $16.95

To order, call 1-877-NEW-WRLD

One Witch's Way
A Magical Year of Stories, Spells & Such

Bronwynn Forrest Torgerson

The Wheel of the Year is given a fresh spin in this inspiring ode to the Wiccan life. Month by month, Bronwynn Forrest Torgerson invigorates Pagan principles with rituals, songs, spells, and poetry. But the underlying thread of this whimsical Wiccan tapestry is Torgerson's own personal stories—funny, enthralling, and moving—that illuminate one Witch's way.

This rich collection offers spiritual lessons, belly laughs, and heartfelt wisdom to Witches everywhere. Mingling the practical and the personal, Torgerson explores journeys in January, love and transformation in February, communion in June, and the power of song in September. Between lyrical verses and original parables, you'll witness the author's joys, struggles, minor miracles, and thrilling encounters with the Divine. From the mundane (magickally finding the perfect apartment) to the mystical (receiving guidance from the gods), Torgerson recounts the sacred forces that have shaped one Witch's life.

978-0-7387-1369-4
240 pp., 6 x 9 $15.95

To order, call 1-877-NEW-WRLD
Prices subject to change without notice

To Write to the Author

If you wish to contact the author or would like more information about this book, please write to the author in care of Llewellyn Worldwide and we will forward your request. Both the author and publisher appreciate hearing from you and learning of your enjoyment of this book and how it has helped you. Llewellyn Worldwide cannot guarantee that every letter written to the author can be answered, but all will be forwarded. Please write to:

Victoria Hunt
c/o Llewellyn Worldwide
2143 Wooddale Drive, Dept. 978-0-7387-1377-9
Woodbury, MN 55125-2989, U.S.A.

Please enclose a self-addressed stamped envelope for reply,
or $1.00 to cover costs. If outside the U.S.A., enclose an
international postal reply coupon.

Many of Llewellyn's authors have websites with additional information and resources. For more information, please visit our website at:

www.llewellyn.com